The Good Life

HENRY JACOBSEN

VICTOR BOOKS

a division of SP Publications, Inc.

WHEATON. ILLINOIS 60187

ISBN 0-88207-018-5
Library of Congress Catalog No. 68-11556

© 1968, Scripture Press Publications, Inc.
World rights reserved. Printed in the United States of America.

Eighth printing, 1977

VICTOR BOOKS
A division of SP Publications, Inc.
P.O. Box 1825 • Wheaton, Illinois 60187

To Marion Leach Jacobsen,
my dear wife and fellow laborer,
this book is dedicated
with appreciation and affection.

Versions Used

Unless otherwise noted, Scripture quotations are from the *New American Standard Bible* (NASB), © The Lockman Foundation, 1960, 1962, 1963, 1968, 1971, 1972, 1973. Other versions used are the King James Version (KJV); *The New Berkeley Version in Modern English* (BERK), © 1969 by the Zondervan Publishing House; *The New Testament in Modern English* (PH), © by J. B. Phillips, published by The Macmillan Company; *The New Testament in the Language of the People* (WMS), by Charles B. Williams, © 1966 by Edith S. Williams, published by Moody Press. All quotations used by permission.

Acknowledgment

The poem "Indifference," on page 88, is from *The Sorrows of God,* by G. A. Studdert-Kennedy, copyright by Harper & Brothers, and is reprinted by permission of Harper & Row, Publishers, Inc., New York.

Contents

This Book and You   **7**

1   *The Good Life (James 1:1)*   **11**

2   *Patience in Trouble (James 1:2-15)*   **22**

3   *Your Religion and Your Life (James 1:16-27)*   **33**

4   *Love and Partiality (James 2:1-13)*   **44**

5   *Faith and Good Works (James 2:14-26)*   **55**

6   *Christians and Speech (James 3:1-12)*   **66**

7   *Wisdom and Humility (James 3:13—4:10)*   **77**

8   *Taking God into Account (James 4:11—5:6)*   **88**

9   *Patience and the Lord's Return (James 5:7-12)*   **99**

10   *The Power of Prayer (James 5:13-20)*   **110**

This Book and You

Over an ice-dispensing machine at a service station in a small Midwestern town hangs a sign: "When all else fails, try following the directions."

The type of study for which this book is designed will be new to most users. For this reason, it is *essential* that you take the time to master this page and the next. To ignore these pages will greatly lessen the value of the course.

In reading this volume, STOP each time you come to a subhead—a line of boldface type dividing the text into sections. Read from your Bible the Scripture passage referred to in the subhead. *Then* go on to read the comment that follows the heading. (In unit 1, which is introductory, a Scripture reference is given with only one subhead.)

Scattered throughout the text you will find numbered blank spaces. At each such space, STOP. Don't read any farther until you have answered the question that precedes the space. Think about the question and then *write your answer* to it in the space. Use either a pencil with a soft, sharp lead, or a ballpoint pen. (The ink from fountain or cartridge pens may blur.)

In writing your answers, be brief. Don't be concerned about complete sentences or even good diction. Use the fewest possible words to express your ideas. For instance, you might answer question 1 (p. 11) by writing:

> *time, money, to go where I've wanted to go,*
> *be able to read, to enjoy my hobby, catch*
> *up on sleep*

Here is the all-important rule for using this book: *Never read beyond the blank space until AFTER you have written your answer to the question that precedes the space*

So that you'll not be tempted to "cheat," you may want to cover the page, below the blank, with a sheet of paper or a 3″ x 5″ file card.

There are at least three ways in which you can use this study book to advantage:

1. In your personal study, either in preparation for a class session or "on your own." Follow the above directions, writing (or at least thinking about) the answer to each question before you read beyond the numbered space. (The numbers are for convenience in identifying the questions.)

2. In group study, in preparation for class. Instead of working alone, as suggested above, study the text in company with your husband, your wife, or one or two other members of the class. Sit around a table and read the text together. When you come to a subhead, have someone read the indicated Scripture. When you come to a blank, discuss the question. But when you write your answer, you need not agree with those with whom you study. Write *your own* answer, especially if a matter of opinion is involved. (Naturally, you *may* agree with the others in the group!)

3. If your children are teen-agers, particularly midteens or older, you may want to use this book for family devotions or family Bible study. Read the Scripture referred to as you come to each subhead, and stop at the blanks to discuss the questions before you read farther. Teen-agers will enjoy talking about the questions, applying the truth, and disagreeing with their parents.

Writing the answers to the questions will force you to think things through. This helpful discipline will make your study far more meaningful than would otherwise be the case. If you simply cannot bring yourself to *write* answers, however, at least form a definite answer in your mind before you read beyond the question and into the next paragraph.

Keep in mind, as you study, that spiritual growth is not merely a matter of knowing what is in the Bible. It depends, instead, on how well you obey what you know. Obedience, not knowledge, is the test of true spirituality—though, of course, you must know God's will before you can obey it.

Pay particular attention, then, to the *Think and Do* section of each unit. If you want this study to result in a genuine personal spiritual experience, actually carry out the suggestions offered there, or those to which the Holy Spirit leads you. If you will *live* God's truth—instead of merely *studying* it—there is almost no limit to the effect the Epistle of James could have on your development, as a Christian, in the good life.

My prayers for each of you as we fellowship in His grace!

HENRY JACOBSEN

THE GOOD LIFE

James 1:1

Before you begin the study of this book, it is of UTMOST
IMPORTANCE *that you familiarize yourself with pages 7-9.*

People often talk about "the good life"—a term you will want to
keep in mind as you study the Epistle of James. Folks use this
expression to refer to the sort of life they would choose to lead—
a life that would eliminate as many as possible of "the heartaches and the thousand natural shocks that flesh is heir to." The
good life is the life they think would give them a minimum of
pain and a maximum of pleasure and fulfilled dreams.

Think for a few minutes. What are the things that would make
life really "good" for *you?* Finish this sentence:

So far as I am concerned, the good life is

(1)

You would probably get a different definition of "the good
life" from every person you questioned. Perhaps there is something, however, that all the definitions would have in common.
Look at what *you* have written. Did you describe the life you
are currently leading—the place where you are living, the work
you are doing, the friends you now have? Most people don't!
The good life, to an average person, is quite unlike his present
existence. The proverb, "The grass is always greener on the other

side of the fence," calls attention to the truism that most people crave what they don't have.

A person with limited income is likely to associate the good life with plenty of money and with freedom from financial worries. A person with a big income and heavy responsibilities may think of the good life in terms of a less complicated existence.

An interior decorator was working in the home of a wealthy family. Around him were all the trappings of luxurious living. The expensive furniture had been imported from Europe. Priceless paintings hung on the walls. There were household servants for the adults and a governess for the two pampered children. The lady of the establishment was dallying with breakfast in bed at the comfortable hour of 11:00 A.M. The decorator, as he worked just outside her bedroom door, could not help overhearing her words.

"Marie," snapped Mrs. Wealthy to her personal maid, in a tone of complete frustration, "I am really so bored with life that I don't know *what* to do. I wish—I wish I could come down with the mumps!"

Madame didn't know, in spite of all her advantages, how to achieve the good life. (Our studies in James will tell you how to acquire the wisdom a person needs to lead a *satisfying* life.)

As we have seen, we usually think of the good life in terms of desirable things we do not now have. What are some other considerations that might enter into making life good?

One element, for instance, might be *geographical*. Most of us would like to live in a climate neither too hot nor too cold. We would not want the weather to be too wet, but neither would we choose to have it so dry that vegetation would be brown most of the year. Those of us who live where the country is uninterestingly flat would perhaps prefer a more scenic area, with mountains, lakes, or rivers to beautify the view.

Circumstances are important, too. To enjoy life completely, we would want to be healthy and free from physical and other handicaps. No hearing aids, spectacles (even contact lenses), or dentures, please! And we would want to have time to do the things we enjoy, and an income adequate to indulge our hobbies, from collecting teacups to raising Shetland ponies.

People are important in the good life. "Birds of a feather flock together," and so some communities cater to special groups. Thousands of older people have moved to Sun City, Arizona, because they like to be near other senior citizens. And many Christians live in the "all-Christian community" called Bibletown in Boca Raton, Florida, because to them the good life is, in part, a matter of being surrounded by others "of like precious faith."

A greater number of individuals, perhaps, find their social needs completely met in a small circle of congenial friends or even in one person—a wife, husband, or friend—who is "special" to them.

This does not mean that we are justified in cultivating only those people who give us pleasure. (You may be surprised by what James has to say about people who "play favorites.")

One's *occupation* is another important element of the good life. Some people like to keep busy. They shrink from the thought of retirement to a life of indolence. Others long to spend an indefinite time doing as little as possible. Some want nothing better than to sit and think. Others would prefer just to sit, period.

Different Notions of the Good Life
Jot down briefly what each of the following persons might think of if asked to define the good life:

1. Mrs. Jones is a frail young woman who lives in a modest suburb. Her husband, by moonlighting, makes barely enough to keep the family financially afloat. Their four children, all under eight years of age, are pushing her to the limits of her endurance. (2)

2. Mr. Brown, 45, has a routine clerical job. He is never comfortable in a group. He has been sick a good deal, feels personally unattractive, and thinks that he cannot hold his own in conversa-

tion. He has never married and lives with his aged mother.
(3)

3. Miss Smith, 28, a schoolteacher, keenly appreciates art, music, and literature. She boards with a dull family in a dreary small town, and knows no one who has any interest in cultural pursuits. Her acquaintances think she is putting on airs, and they seem to make a point of excluding her.
(4)

What Is the Truly Good Life?

God wants His creatures to lead rich, satisfying lives. Jesus said, in speaking of His followers, "I came to bring them life, and far more life than before" (John 10:10, PH). God has made it possible for His people to have "life that is life indeed." Eternal (or spiritual) life has a three-dimensional quality completely lacking in the lives of those who are not Christians. Unbelievers have only the life of the body and soul (or mind). They lack the life of the spirit—the capacity for fellowship, now and forever, with God.

Just how do Christians differ from non-Christians?

First, write your own personal definition of a Christian:
(5)

Maybe you defined a Christian as a person who believes in Jesus Christ. This is a standard definition. But what does it *mean* to "believe" in Jesus Christ? Believing is much more than simply subscribing to a set of doctrinal statements. The belief that makes a person a Christian includes the element of commitment. A Christian is a person who not only *knows* the Gospel and *believes* it is true, but has *committed* himself to it.

Such a person, in effect, has said to God, "Lord, I know there is nothing about me that makes me worthy of Your love, but I know You love me anyway. I know it because I read it in the pages of Your Book, the Bible. I believe that Your love led You to send Your Son to earth to die on the cross for my sin. I'm not trusting in my own character or in anything 'good' that I can do. I believe that Jesus paid the penalty for my sin and I'm trusting You to accept me as Your child because of my confidence in Your promise that whoever believes on Your Son *has* everlasting life" (cf. John 3:36).

A person who takes this humble, trusting attitude toward God becomes God's child (John 1:12) as he receives Christ as his Saviour. He becomes a member of God's family (Gal. 4:6, 7) and a sharer in God's nature (2 Peter 1:4). God gives him *eternal* life. This is not only unending life, but is—here and now—an entirely *different* kind of life, far superior to mere *physical* life. It is *the good life.*

Much confusion arises because some people think being a Christian is merely a matter of believing that certain things are true. Right belief *is* essential, of course—because if we do not believe that the facts of the Gospel are true, we are likely to ignore them. But, as we shall see in our study of James, it is entirely possible to believe all the right doctrines without being a Christian. Christian faith naturally includes believing the truth, but it *also* includes the all-important element of *trust,* or *commitment* to truth, and the vital ingredient of. *obedience* to truth. James has a lot to say about how a genuine Christian differs from a professing Christian (one who merely *says* he is a believer).

The Good Life That God Offers You
Most people think about the good life in terms of things and circumstances, but God does not link *His* good life with "things" at all. Jesus said, to a man who wanted Him to settle a family financial dispute, "Look out and be on guard against all greed, for one's life is not made up of the abundance of his possessions"

(Luke 12:15, BERK). The truly good life is not a matter of posessions, popularity, health, good looks, and the like. It has to do not so much with what one *has* as with what one IS. Its foundation is one's personal relationship with God through trust in Christ, without which one cannot be a Christian or experience God's good life.

Do all the Christians you know seem to be *enjoying* this good life? Are they happy and satisfied? Do they revel in their relationship with God?

(6)

Probably your answer was an emphatic "No!" Maybe you yourself have received Christ as your Saviour but are still far from having what you could honestly call a satisfying life. List two or three attitudes that seem to keep some Christians from conscious enjoyment of the more abundant life—the rich, full, satisfying life God wants His creatures to have:

(7)

Did you include worry? Worry (or fear) can take the joy out of life. Most of us can find things to worry about. Getting the right job, saving for the down payment on a house, buying a new car, finding the right church, getting ahead in one's career, beating the high cost of living, office problems, the difficulties of bringing up children, problems of personal health, having unpleasant neighbors, dread of old age—to say nothing of the crime wave, today's great upsurge of immorality, and the precarious international situation—these are only a few of the things one can worry about.

It is simply not true that *Christians* have nothing to be concerned over. Anyone who embraces Christianity to avoid his share of trouble is due for disappointment. God doesn't promise that His people will go soaring to heaven on "flow'ry beds of ease." He doesn't assure them they won't have their quota of accidents, illness, disappointments, and problems.

In Spite of Trouble—the Good Life

One wonderful thing about God's good life is that it doesn't depend on freedom from trouble and affliction. Thousands of Christians have learned from experience that one can have a full, rich, abundantly "good" life under circumstances that, humanly speaking, are completely intolerable. Regardless of your income, your social position, your occupation, or your health, you may enjoy God's good life *without a change in your circumstances.*

Some Christians have been totally blind or otherwise handicapped, or have spent long years on sickbeds, and yet have radiated a joy and contentment that has amazed all who knew them. They have not been putting on an act, either. Their happiness has been genuine. They have found life *good*—not because of pleasant circumstances and surroundings, but because of their relationship with God. This relationship, the most wonderful thing in life, has enabled them to see themselves and their problems as God sees them.

John and Jerry are young men. John has committed himself to the Lord. He is trusting Christ and is rejoicing in his relationship with Him. Jerry has never made such a commitment. He attends church now and then, but he feels no vital relationship with God. When these two men face trouble, why is it easier for John to come through with flying colors?

(8)

Maybe you wrote that John is happier because he knows he is going to heaven. It is true that the prospect of eternity with God lifts one over life's hard spots. But John has another big advantage. He has the reassuring confidence that here and now, *in this life,* the Lord Jesus is his Companion and Friend. God is with John in all his troubles (Isa. 43:1-2). All God's infinite resources—wisdom, strength, courage, consolation, guidance—are at a believer's disposal. You will find that conscious awareness of the Lord's presence in trying experiences can be as great a comfort as the prospect of heaven at the end of this life. (James wrote his epistle to Christians who were undergoing all kinds of difficult testings, and his advice is as good today as it was in the first century. He even has a word for those believers who, in hard times, are planning for the future—a word that will help to minimize possible disappointments.)

Why Christianity Is Unreal to Some People

But not everyone who calls himself a Christian is comforted by the prospect of heaven or encouraged by a sense of God's presence. The outlook of entirely too many Christians is very similar to the outlook of their unbelieving friends. They see life pretty much as the rest of the world sees it. There is no real difference in their attitudes and conduct. Their religious profession or belief just doesn't affect the way they think and act.

Try this test. Ask yourself these questions about your Christian friends—those who attend church faithfully:

When they are together socially, do they talk freely and with pleasure about God, the Bible, or their spiritual experiences? If not, *why not?*

(9)

Knowledge of Bible truth, as James tells us, is in itself useless, though it *is* the first step toward God's good life. Do your Christian friends have family Bible *study?* Personal Bible *study?* Do they memorize Scripture? If not, *why not?*

(10)

James has something to say, in his letter, about why we don't get answers to prayer. Many people don't get answers because they don't pray. How about your Christian friends—do they pray systematically? Do they *ever* spend time in prayer when they are together socially? If not, *why not?*
(11)

Now go over those last three questions again. This time answer them for *yourself*. You needn't *write* your answers this time—but face the facts!

Do you honestly think most Christians *want* God's good life enough to *do* something about it? If not, *why not?*
(12)

And how about *you?* Do *you* really want it? If not, *why not?*
(13)

The world's so-called good life is for the favored few. It depends on what one has, on who and where one is. It rests on circumstances, which may change overnight.

But God's good life—the only *truly* good life—is for all who will take it. It does not depend on who you know or what you have. It rests squarely upon your relationship with an unchanging God who is all-powerful, all-knowing, and all-loving. No temporal circumstances, no misfortune, no opposition can deprive you of *this* good life (Rom. 8:38-39). That's *God's* promise!

The Epistle of James and the Good Life (James 1:1)
The Epistle of James is one of the most practical, hard-hitting books in the Bible. It will show you what is involved in being a

genuine believer—a person who has access to the truly good life.

The epistle does not describe "the good life" as such, or tell us how to achieve it. If, however, you pattern your life by the truths of this book, you will find yourself *living* "the good life." This life is good because God is at its center; He shapes everything within its circumference. This is the life that yields happiness and satisfaction about which a person can know nothing if his goal is merely possessions, pleasure, or personal achievement.

The Hebrew Christians to whom James wrote had been driven out of Palestine. They'd lost their jobs, their homes, and most of their possessions. They were in many cases separated from friends and family. They had had to make a new start among hostile people in unfamiliar places. We would call them refugees or displaced persons; they suffered all that these modern terms imply. They lived from hand to mouth. They were hated by the Jews because in becoming Christians they had deserted the faith of their fathers, and by the Romans because they were loyal to a King other than Caesar.

James, who wrote this epistle, was probably a half-brother of the Lord Jesus Christ. It seems that he didn't believe in Jesus during our Lord's lifetime (cf. John 7:5), but was converted soon after the Resurrection. He became a person of importance in the Early Church. He presided over the first Church Council, held in Jerusalem about A.D. 49 and recorded in Acts 15. For all his position and authority, however, James modestly refers to himself as the bond-servant, or slave, of his illustrious Brother and of God.

The Epistle of James was one of the first books of the New Testament to be put into writing, perhaps around A.D. 45. The writer addresses himself to "the twelve tribes who are dispersed abroad" (v. 1). This "dispersion" isn't the one caused by the Romans after they had destroyed Jerusalem in A.D. 70. Rather, James had in mind the scattering abroad of Jewish Christians in the persecution that followed Stephen's martyrdom in A.D. 32 (Acts 8:1). The "twelve tribes" were those Jews from any of the Hebrew tribes who had been converted to Christian faith.

Think and Do

What is God's "good life"? To what group of people is it restricted? Do you qualify for it on the ground of a right relationship to God? If not, what will you do to qualify? If you qualify, how will you help *someone else* to do likewise? If you know someone who should be taking this course, will you bring him to the next session?

PATIENCE IN TROUBLE

James 1:2-15

"Blessed is a man who perseveres under trial; for once he has been approved, he will receive the crown of life, which the Lord has promised to those who love Him" (James 1:12).

A wide variety of troubles overtake people—everything from poor health to rebellious adolescents, from financial reverses to difficult neighbors or in-laws. Jot down, in a word or two each, the four troubles or problems most common among people you know: (14)

If you have problems (and who doesn't?), there's a message for you in James 1. Here's a philosophy of trouble as down-to-earth as the trials you face. Some people have missed the help of this biblical advice because they haven't tried it. And many haven't tried it because they don't know about it.

How to Be Happy though Miserable (James 1:2-4)

God doesn't expect you to *enjoy* trouble (cf. v. 2). He knows you are a human being, with human feelings. But He wants you to "consider it all joy" when troubles come your way. You can actually be happy in testings if you know God is using trouble to bring about His purposes in, for, or through you. If you have done something wrong, God may use trials to bring your sin to your attention so that you will repent and stop whatever displeases Him. But troubles often come even to those who aren't deliberately doing wrong.

Remember that God is sovereign. He is completely in control of this universe and of everything (and everyone) in it. When something "goes wrong," either God *causes* it or He *allows* it. In either case, He *uses* what happens and through it brings about His good, acceptable, and perfect will.

One result that God wants to produce in you through trials is suggested in verse 3: "The testing of your faith produces *endurance*." This seems, at first glance, like a rather dubious kind of blessing. It suggests that your trials are sent to give you ability to endure *more* trials. But endurance includes strength, virility, and resilience—qualities useful in all areas of life. You need such endurance to face professional demands, domestic responsibilities and stresses, a routine office job, church work, or the difficult task of bringing up a family.

Officer candidates in the Air Force undergo grueling training. For the first six weeks they get only a few hours' sleep a night. They are pushed to the limit of physical endurance and are subjected to constant disagreeable "harassment." As a result, "the men are separated from the boys." A sizeable percentage of the candidates drop out, unable to stand the strain. Those who remain, however, develop endurance. They also acquire poise, bearing, leadership ability, and personal competence—qualities that will be invaluable to them in *any* career, military or civilian, that they later follow.

In the spiritual realm, too, "endurance" (called "patience" in the KJV), will eventually have its "perfect result." You will become mature, "without any defects" (WMS), prepared to face with confidence whatever comes your way. You will lack nothing you need for the good life. And so your trials, even if they are disagreeable for a time, will at last be eminently worthwhile.

When troubles come, it is perfectly normal for you to wish that God would change your circumstances to suit you. God's usual practice, however, is to change you to suit your circumstances. He will "equip you in every good thing to do His will" (cf. Heb. 13:21). By preparing you to face trouble and the constant strains of life, God enables you to rise above your circumstances and to live victoriously and to His glory.

Why do you think most Christians do *not* consider it all joy when they face troubles and afflictions?
(15)

James suggests one reason for inability to be joyful in trials. Some young men in college would sooner indulge lazy habits, sleep late, overeat, and smoke or drink, than train for an athletic team. Such youths sacrifice whatever potential they have for becoming good athletes. Some Christians, likewise, are more interested in present comfort and material prosperity than in becoming well developed, mature men and women who will be useful in God's service and a blessing to others. They lack "wisdom" (v. 5) for responding to their trials as God wants them to. Do *you* lack such wisdom?

The Lord, who allows you to meet troubles that will shape you into what you ought to be, is ready to give you wisdom to respond to your trials in such a way that they will more quickly accomplish His purposes. He may not take away your trials, but He will give you victory over them, peace of heart and mind in the midst of them, and awareness that in meeting them you are developing spiritual strength, learning to trust God more fully, and becoming more like Christ. Don't minimize the importance of these results!

Why We Don't Know How to Meet Trouble (James 1:5-8)
Don't overlook one little detail about God's giving you wisdom. You must ask Him for it trustingly (v. 5). Christians often do not get something because they do not ask for it (4:2). It never occurs to them, apparently, that God definitely promises to give them, at their request, all the wisdom they need to meet life's

trials. But they must ask for it "in faith."

In your own words, what does it mean to "ask in faith" (v. 6)?
(16)

Some people want to test God. "Show me," they tell Him, "and I'll believe You." But man cannot demand that God prove Himself. God says, "Believe Me, and I'll show you." Men say, "Seeing is believing." God says, "Believing [trusting] leads to seeing." Jesus said, "Be it done to you according to your faith" (Matt. 9:29). A person with faith *expects* God to answer him.

James compares a doubter to a wave of the ocean, driven and tossed by the wind (v. 6, KJV). How does a person who doubts God resemble a wave?
(17)

A person who doubts is "a double-minded man, unstable in all his ways" (v. 8). He is like a pasture gate that swings both ways in the wind. Now it is open this way and now that, and sometimes it is shut. A doubter may "believe" at times, but at other times he *doesn't* believe, and he is never quite sure. A double-minded man doesn't even know for certain what he *wants*. He would like to succeed in his career, but he also wants to take life easy. He wants to have his daily Quiet Time with the Lord, but he likes to sleep late mornings. He wants to lose weight, but he also wants that second helping of mashed potatoes. He wants the Lord to use him, but he'd like to cling to his indifferent, careless, unspiritual habits.

John Harris, 25, is a faithful member of a church where the Gospel is preached. A few years ago he professed personal faith in Christ. He worries because he has not yet found the woman he would like to marry. He tells his pastor about his problem. The pastor says, "The Lord knows all about you and is perfectly able to bring you and the right woman together if marriage is His will for you." John says, "Pastor, how I *wish* I could believe that! But I just *can't*."

If you were John Harris' pastor, what would you tell him? (18)

Did you tell John how to find a girl or tell him how faith comes?

There are two principal sources of faith, and the first one is the Bible. "Faith comes from hearing what is told, and hearing through the message about Christ" (Rom. 10:17, wms). There is no better way to develop vigorous faith than to read the Bible with open mind, expecting God to speak to you through it. Learn God's promises and the glorious things He has done in the past, remembering that by definition God cannot change—He *must* be "the same yesterday and today, yes and forever" (Heb. 13:8). Foolish men may mourn the death of their so-called god, but this betrays their lack of personal experience with the God who is life. God is supreme; He is concerned for His people; He answers prayer. The better you get to know Him, through the Bible, the more trustingly you will pray to Him.

Faith also comes through experience—your own and that of others. As you learn how God has helped other Christians, you will be able to depend on Him for yourself—and as you experience answered prayer, you will find it increasingly easy to trust Him as new problems arise.

Remember that faith is not a matter of the feelings, or emotions. Your feelings depend on how you slept, your general health, and the circumstances in which you find yourself. Faith, on the other hand, is a matter of the *will*—the part of your personality that makes decisions. You can actually make up your mind to trust God if you *want* to. People who say they *want* to believe, but *can't*, simply do not understand what faith really is.

Suppose you were lost in a deserted section of a strange city and asked an extremely shifty-looking individual to direct you to your destination. Having received his instructions, you would have to decide whether you would trust him or not. You probably would not *feel* like trusting him—but regardless of your feelings, you *could* exercise faith in him by simply following his directions and, hopefully, getting to your destination.

Even if you do not *feel* like trusting God (and even if you do not feel that you *are* trusting Him), you can make up your mind, or *decide,* to do so. If you really *want* to trust God, JUST DO IT. Tell Him, if you can do so sincerely, that you are ready to trust Him. If necessary, say, "Lord, I don't *feel* that I am trusting You. In fact, I feel *scared.* But I have *decided* to trust You *and I am doing so."* And act on your trust by believing and acting on God's promises and by obeying His Word, the Bible.

Suppose you need wisdom—to face a trial or to make a decision. Ask for it, expecting to receive it. Then believe that God *has answered* your prayer. After all, He has promised to! Consider all the factors involved in the situation that confronts you and, depending on God for guidance, use your best judgment and make your decision—and believe that God led you to it!

Wisdom in Accepting Material Circumstances (James 1:9-11)
You may well need wisdom in developing a right attitude toward material possessions. Old Testament Jews were inclined to look on wealth as evidence of God's blessing, and some people cling to this notion even today. James has some rather surprising remarks on the subject. (He is quite outspoken about some rich people, as you'll see in later studies.)

If you are poor, you are to glory in your *high* position (v. 9). James was writing to and about *Christians.* Even if a Christian is poor, he has God, and because he has God, he has everything that matters most. Have you ever sung, "My Father is rich in houses and lands; He holdeth the wealth of the world in His hands . . . I'm a child of the King"? No doubt there are times when you forget the truth expressed in this song. If your worldly circumstances are humble, you may even worry or be unhappy. Remember that a century from now—and maybe a lot sooner—

it won't matter a bit how much money you have in the bank today, how large a home is covered by your mortgage, or the kind of car on which you are making payments. But it will matter tremendously that you were a child of God through faith in His Son.

If you're a Christian who has material wealth, on the other hand, don't boast about your money, but glory in your "humiliation" (v. 10). Recognize that no matter how much you have, you can't take it into eternity with you. You can *rejoice* in this humiliation because—though you cannot carry your wealth to heaven—you, by virtue of your trust in Christ, may be serenely confident of your personal salvation and your eternal riches.

Wealth is a plant that flourishes until the hot sun of adversity and the dry wind of financial reverses strike it. Then it withers away (v. 11). List a few of the things, besides money, which men treasure but which do not last:
(19)

What did you write? Did you mention *youth*—a commodity held in much esteem by this generation? How about *beauty, health, popularity, fame, authority* (or *power*), *social position,* and *business success?* All these are highly valued, if not almost worshiped. But they are here today and gone forever tomorrow. People—Christians or otherwise—who look to these things for lasting satisfaction are facing a sad awakening. As Thomas Gray said,

> The boast of heraldry, the pomp of power,
>   And all that beauty, all that wealth e'er gave,
> Await alike th' inevitable hour:
>   The paths of glory lead but to the grave.

Sometimes Temptations Are Our Trials (James 1:12-15)
Some of the testings that come your way regularly, no doubt, are temptations to do wrong. In fact, the same Greek word

means both "trial" (vv. 2, 3, 12) and "temptation" (cf. vv. 12-15). Temptation can be one of life's greatest troubles, and since Jesus Himself faced temptation (Matt. 4:1-10), it is not likely that a mere human being will escape it. Ask yourself: "What special temptations have confronted me in the past week? What temptations do I face more or less regularly?"

To begin with, it is no sin to be tempted. If it were, Jesus would be a sinner, for *He* was tempted. The sin lies in *yielding* to temptation and doing the wrong to which you are enticed. There is a proverb, "You can't keep the birds from flying over your head, but you don't have to let them nest in your hair." You can't help being tempted—but you don't *have* to *yield*. And you don't *have* to welcome tempting thoughts into your mind, toy with them, and enjoy thinking them.

God is completely holy; sin has no attraction for Him. He doesn't tempt anyone (v. 13). He allows you to be tempted— but He does not tempt you with a view to leading you into sin. Nor does He tempt you in order to learn how faithful you are. He knows in advance how you will react to temptation, for He knows *all* things:

After you have read verse 14, write briefly, in your own words, why sin is so attractive to us:

(20)

Verses 14 and 15 suggest this established pattern:

1. Our "lust"—the desire of the flesh nature—inclines us to do evil.

2. We are carried away by our passions, or sinful impulses.

3. Our lust gives birth to wrong acts, or sins.

4. The outcome of sin is spiritual death (eternal separation from God).

So don't blame God for temptation. God is on your side when you are enticed to do wrong, for "no temptation has overtaken you but such as is common to man; and God is faithful, who will not allow you to be tempted beyond what you are able, but with the temptation will provide the way of escape also, that you may be able to endure it" (1 Cor. 10:13).

Actually, you yield to temptation because, though you may *want* to resist sin and do the right thing, you *feel* like doing wrong, and so you *decide* to go ahead and *do* the wrong thing to which you are tempted. When temptation comes, you *could* —if you *really made up your mind* to do so—resist it and overcome it. If you are vitally related to God through personal faith in Christ, the Holy Spirit who indwells you makes it possible for you to overcome temptation in the strength of God Himself.

How does a person usually feel after a time of severe trial, or after he has yielded to temptation?

(21)

On the other hand, you'll find that *resisting* temptation— closing your mind to it and *refusing* to yield to it—will help you overcome future temptation. "Each vict'ry will help you some other to win."

It is quite normal, when trouble comes or you have succumbed to temptation, to feel discouraged. You may ask yourself, at such times, "If God really loved me, would He allow this to happen to me? It must be that God doesn't care about me, or that He can't do anything to help me. So what's the use of my trying, anyway?

Of course this is not the attitude for a believer to take! James tells us, in a verse which nicely concludes our study of this unit, "Blessed [happy] is a man who perseveres under trial; for once he has been approved, he will receive the crown of life, which the Lord has promised to those who love Him" (James 1:12). There is a heavenly reward for those who love God and show their love by patiently enduring trials and temptations. There is an element of testing in the troubles God allows to come your way, and you can win His approval by enduring them. To persevere is just the opposite of giving up. Discouragement leads to despair, but perseverance leads to victory and happiness. God rewards, with the crown of life, those who remain faithful under trials. We don't know exactly what is involved in this heavenly reward, but you may be certain that getting the Lord's crown of life will make all your trials infinitely worth whatever they have cost.

Remember, though, that reward in heaven is by no means all that God offers you. The satisfaction of overcoming trials and temptations is a potent reward in the living present and yields a rich quota of present satisfaction.

Dealing with Troubles as They Come (Summary)

Let's "wrap up" briefly what you have learned about enduring trials (and resisting temptations):

1. God is using trials to develop your endurance and to lead you toward personal spiritual maturity.

2. God will supply the wisdom you need in dealing with trials or other problems. *Expect* Him to supply your need—and then *act accordingly*.

3. For a Christian, "high position" is not a matter of possessing wealth but of being God's child through faith in Christ.

4. Even when appearances are to the contrary, believe God loves you—if you are trusting Him—and that He is giving you strength and guidance.

5. Don't allow your feelings to discourage you. Faith is based on God's unfailing love and power, not on your changing feelings. Decide once and for all to believe God's promises, and then ignore your feelings.

Some people will say, "I *tried* all that and it didn't work. Don't give me those pat, easy answers! It's not that simple!"

It is true that victory over life's trials is not always simple—especially for people who refuse to admit that the plain statements of Scripture mean just what they say. Don't judge or condemn such people—but keep in mind that when you must choose between the promises of God and the personal experiences of men and women, you should not find the decision too difficult to make.

Think and Do

What is your greatest trial right now? Do you insist that God remove it, or are you willing for Him to equip you to live with it?

What needed qualities could God be developing in you through this trial? How are you accepting the lesson He is teaching you?

What will be your attitude toward trials? Will you rejoice because God is using trouble to make you the person He wants you to be?

YOUR RELIGION AND YOUR LIFE

James 1:16-27

"This is pure and undefiled religion in the sight of our God and Father, to visit orphans and widows in their distress, and to keep oneself unstained by the world" (James 1:27).

If someone asked you for a one-sentence definition of "religion," what would you tell him?
(22)

The dictionary gives at least four definitions of *religion.* The word as used in James 1:27 usually refers to the forms and ceremonies involved in the worship of God. A "religious" person is one who is careful about meeting with others for instruction, worship, and the Lord's Supper, and who reads the Bible and prays. One would probably call such a person a good church member. Not every religious person, or church member, is necessarily a *Christian,* but every Christian surely ought to be faithful in his worship and devotional practices.

Unfortunately, some people seem to think that "religion" is *all* God wants of people. They confuse church membership or participation in the forms of worship—both of which have a rightful claim on our attention—with salvation, which is a matter of right relationship to God. In Old Testament days, the most *religious* people—the priests and the Levites—were sometimes the greatest rascals, and there are always people who use "religion" as a disguise. Behind all their religious acts they hide sinful habits or an utter lack of reality in their spiritual experience.

James 1 points out that "pure religion" (v. 27) involves at least four elements: recognition of God as the Source of all good (James 1:16-18), the exercise of self-control (vv. 19-21), obedience to the Bible (vv. 22-25), and personal purity and helpfulness to others (vv. 26-27).

Recognizing God as the Giver of All Good (James 1:16-18)

Don't be misled (v. 16) by the erroneous idea that God is the Source of temptation. Far from being responsible for temptation (v. 13), God is the Source of the *good* things that make life pleasant and worthwhile (v. 17).

What are some of God's "gifts" to mankind?

(23)

Go over your list and underline the gifts God has given *you*.

It may be pushing the text a bit far, but some people distinguish between God's "good" gifts and His "perfect" gifts (cf. kjv). They apply the adjective "good" to gifts in which most people share, and they reserve the term "perfect" for spiritual gifts that are limited to Christians. "Good" gifts, then, would include life itself, normal physical and mental faculties, husbands or wives, children, friends, a supply of such necessities of life as shelter, clothing, food, water, and work; such endowments as ability to reason; and such special talents as musical or artistic ability, etc.

"Perfect" gifts would include salvation, assurance, fellowship with God and His people, and the special gifts listed in passages like Ephesians 4 and 1 Corinthians 12.

Tom is a "self-made" man. Unable to afford college, he took

a job and applied himself. He studied nights and did the work of two men—and did it well. He is now in a managerial position in which he makes good use of his natural leadership ability. He is married to a beautiful girl and they have three lovely children. "I made it by working hard," says Tom modestly. "God did nothing for me!" Why is Tom wrong?

(24)

For one thing, where did Tom get his ambition to improve himself, which is not at all a common gift? Where did he get his ability to lead others and the stamina that enabled him to work so hard? He can claim no credit for these qualities, with which he was born. Such traits are God's "good" gifts.

Did someone you are fond of ever stop caring for you? Has a friend ever "knifed" you behind your back? Has a loved one proved unfaithful? Have you ever heard of children losing their respect and affection for their parents? Most of us have had or heard of these experiences, which grow out of human lack of constancy. But God is unchanging (Heb. 13:8). With Him there is no variation (James 1:17). He is faithful (1 Cor. 10:13). He is the only One in the whole universe who is always and forever the same. This means that you can depend implicitly on God. He will never cease to love you. The "good life," in essence, is your unchanging relationship to this unchanging Person.

We sometimes call this relationship salvation. As verse 18 suggests, it is God's greatest and most perfect *gift*. You don't earn it or deserve it—it originates in God and comes about through "the exercise of His will." It is God's idea and He does everything to make it available to you.

Some parents buy a child several things to give him for Christmas or on his birthday. After he has received the lesser presents, they give him *the* gift of the occasion—something more expensive and "special." They "save the best for last." But God's policy is to give us His greatest and most perfect gift *first*. Salvation, through which we become God's children by putting our trust in His Son as our Saviour, qualifies us for receiving all God's other "perfect" gifts—the gifts which are only for His people. The means by which God makes salvation available to us is "the Word of truth," which Peter calls "the living and abiding Word of God" (1 Peter 1:23).

The Bible, "the message about Christ" (Rom. 10:17, wms), is "living and active" (Heb. 4:12). As you respond to it in faith —*as you obey it*—the Holy Spirit, who works through it, imparts the life of God to you and you become "a first specimen of His new creation" (ph). All that is involved in that new creation will become apparent only after Christ's return to earth, when He will make all things new (Rev. 21:5) and you will be transformed into His likeness (Phil. 3:21; 1 John 3:2). In the meantime, your *present* life is to be changed—for the better (cf. 2 Cor. 5:17)—as a "sample," or "first-fruits," of what God can and will do.

What are some of the changes most of us need most?
(25)

Exercising Control Over Oneself (James 1:19-21)

James seems almost to apologize for introducing this subject. "You know this" (cf. v. 19), he begins, and then goes on to write about self-control. From your observation or experience, what are some of the unhelpful or wrong things people do if they lack self-control?
(26)

There are three good rules in verse 19. The first rule is, "Be quick to hear," which simply means be ready to listen. The dispositions of a good many people would be improved if they would follow this rule! People are usually so eager to talk—ordinarily about themselves—that it is hard for them to stop long enough to find out what the other person is trying to say. Not all of us are like the woman who greets her friends with, "Say! Didja hear . . . ?" followed by the latest morsel of gossip, but few of us know how to listen as well as we know how to talk.

The mother whose child is trying to explain how the candy dish got broken, the foreman whose worker is telling why the job wasn't done right, the Sunday School teacher whose pupil is telling why he has been absent for three weeks—all these need to learn how to listen sympathetically. Granted we often get poor excuses rather than good reasons, we owe the other person a fair hearing and an opportunity to present his case.

The second rule here is "Be slow to speak," which is the converse of "Be quick to hear." If only we would listen more and better, what we have to say would probably be better, too.

Socially, a person who does all the talking, or most of it, is likely to be known as "the mouth." Surprisingly enough, perhaps, a person who lets other people talk, and who interrupts them only to ask another question, often gets a reputation as a good conversationalist.

Have you ever noticed that the people who talk the most in a group often say the least? There is a place for "small talk"—chitchat about this and that—but most of us could greatly improve our reputations as conversationalists if we would say a lot less. We need to resist the impulse to pass on that bit of confidential information and that derogatory gossip which may be true but certainly is unkind and unnecessary.

The lowest level of conversation is talk about *people*. The second level is talk about *things*—appliances, cars, houses, events, personal experiences. The highest level is talk about *ideas*. Why do most people seldom converse at the top level?

(27)

How could a person go about upgrading the level of his conversation?
(28)

The third rule given by James is, "Be slow to anger." Man's anger does not produce results that are in line with God's righteousness (v. 20). Instead, it wounds people, wrecks friendships and family relationships, and displeases the Lord. If you have a hot temper, don't be proud of it! Memorize verse 20 and repeat it to yourself when you are tempted to "blow your stack."

Jack and Jane are newlyweds. Jack inherited a "volatile" disposition. He is inclined to lose his temper at the drop of a hat. Jane is phlegmatic and easygoing. Both were converted a year ago. Jane never loses her temper, and Jack now loses his only once in a great while. Which of the two has won the greater spiritual victory, and why?
(29)

Lack of self-control is in the same category as filthiness and wickedness (v. 21), which we are to "put aside." God will enable you to do this, but *you* must *decide* to do it. If you were walking through the woods and came to a deep ravine crossed by a frail footbridge, the bridge would get you across the chasm only as you trusted it by walking over it. In a way, God's help is like such a bridge. He helps you only as you make your decision and claim victory by trusting Him and expecting Him to "hold you up."

God's Word is able to save your soul (cf. v. 21). It contains the message of the Gospel, God's provision for man's eternal life, and it is in itself living and energetic (Heb. 4:12). It is the living "seed" by which you may be born again (1 Peter 1:23) into God's family. But unless you are "humble" about yourself, you may not realize how desperately you need God. You may think that you are good enough to "get by," and so miss out entirely on salvation.

You "receive the Word" by believing it, or "trusting" it. As you have seen, you can trust anything or anyone if you make up your mind to, for trust is an act of the *will*. It is *not* primarily a matter of the feelings or the intellect. Determine *now* to trust God and His Word at all costs!

Heeding and Obeying the Word of God (James 1:22-25)
The word "but," with which this paragraph of the passage starts, normally points to a contrast between two ideas. Can you find the two contrasted ideas to which this "but" calls our attention? (30)

The contrast is between "receiving" (v. 21) the Word, or merely hearing it (v. 22), and actually *obeying* it. The importance of this distinction cannot be overemphasized. Often we do not even remember what we have read in the Bible. And how much can you recall of the last sermon you heard? Most of us have wonderful "forgetteries" when it comes to Bible truth!

Then, too, a good many Christians don't realize that merely knowing the Bible is by itself no measure of spirituality. Not knowledge, but *obedience,* is the yardstick of one's spiritual condition. Knowledge is essential, of course—because you can't obey what you don't know—but knowledge without obedience is even worse than worthless. It is downright dangerous, because a person who knows God's will and disobeys it is far worse off than the one who disobeys it through ignorance (Luke 12:46-48).

How can you study the Bible in a way that will help you be a doer of the Word, ready to obey God's revealed will for you? (31)

For one thing, you could notice the *commands* in the passage you read—the verses containing imperative verbs or beginning with "Let us . . ." or a similar construction. Copy these commands in a notebook each day. Make a special effort, with God's help, to obey them.

Mark Twain, who was not a believer, said he had no problem with parts of the Bible that he couldn't understand. The parts that gave him trouble, he said, were those that he understood all too well. You, too, will find that your problem is not with your inability to understand Scripture—it is with your unwillingness to live by the parts that are perfectly clear to you.

The Bible, or God's Word, is like a mirror. You can glance at your reflection in a mirror—in a department store, for instance, or while you are walking along the street, and walk away with no serious thought about the image you have seen. Or, you can look at a mirror closely, as when a man adjusts his tie or combs his hair, or when a girl "primps" before a party.

In much the same way, it is possible for you to read the Bible casually and, when you have finished a chapter, not have the remotest idea of what you have read. Such Bible reading may salve your conscience, but it contributes nothing to your spiritual growth. On the other hand, you can look at the Word "intently" (v. 25), concentrating on what you read and watching for truths that bear on your current needs and problems—your impatience, lack of confidence, domestic troubles, worries about the future, selfishness, discouragement. You can look, in each chapter, for traits to cultivate, sins to avoid, warnings to heed, commands to obey, and promises to claim. Ask yourself, as you read, "What does this chapter teach me about God? About the Saviour? About myself?" If you come to a verse that really "hits" you, stop and think about it. Ask yourself just how you can respond and make that verse real in your experience. Begin *right then,* with God's help, to live by that truth.

Your Bible reading will be far more effective if each day you obey one new truth, as a result of reading a few verses carefully, than if you skim over three or four chapters a day and come to grips with nothing.

A Christian is to live by "the law of liberty" (v. 25). Of course this does not mean he is free to ignore God's requirements of righteousness and holiness. It means that he is free from the curse of the Law. He is at liberty (which an unsaved person is *not*) to follow the leadings of the Spirit of Christ, who indwells him. When God fully controls a man's wishes and desires, that man is literally free to do as he pleases—because his own great desire will be to please God. Such a person will delight (cf. Ps. 40:8) to do God's will—to study and obey the Bible, to live a life of practical godliness, to do what he can to help his family, friends, and neighbors, and to worship God sincerely with heart and soul.

Helping Others and Personal Purity (James 1:26-27)

For all his "religion," a person who can't control his tongue is getting nowhere spiritually. He is deceiving his own heart, but is probably not fooling anyone else. Certainly he is not deceiving God. (We study this subject again in James 3.)

"Pure" religion is more than participation in forms or ceremonies (much as you may find such rites helpful in worshiping God). God accepts the formal worship of those who sincerely adore Him in the pomp of a great cathedral, but the "religion" that most delights God's heart expresses itself in active Christian love, especially toward those who are needy and unable to help themselves (v. 27). Widows in James' day had an unhappy life and were subject to great temptation. Orphans, too, were in dire need of help.

What specific things could *you* do *this week* in the way of helping others? What could you do as the equivalent of "visiting widows and orphans"?

(32)

The Greek word translated "visit" means to inspect with a view to helping (cf. Matt. 25:36; Luke 1:78; Acts 15:14). Even if you are in no position to help anyone financially, certainly there must be someone whom you could help with your sympathy, understanding, or Christian love. Surely you know someone who needs encouragement, comfort, or "cheering up"! Keep in mind that whatever you do for others in Jesus' name, you do for your Lord (Matt. 25:40). In fact, serving others is the *only* way, today, that you can serve Him.

The other thing God wants in the way of "pure religion" is that you keep yourself unspotted by the world. "The world," mentioned five times in James, is the whole order of things in which we live. It is the cultural, economic, social, political, and "religious" set-up of our times. The Bible points out that the world has nothing in common with God. It warns you not to love the world because it is not permanent (1 John 2:15-17).

Even if you do not set your heart on the world, with its materialism, pride of life, and carnality, it is easy to become "stained" by it. You naturally want to be like other people. You do not want to be thought odd. You long for the material success—money and popularity—by which others judge you. First thing you know, God and spiritual interests are in second place. You have been contaminated by the world around you. You have allowed it to "squeeze you into its mold" (cf. Rom. 12:2, PH). You begin to think and act like people to whom God is only an uncomfortable idea.

By yourself, you could never escape the world's defilement, but God can give you higher motives than the people of the world have. He can enable you to keep your heart and mind pure, even when you are sorely tempted to conform to the standards of non-Christian society.

Religion That Is Pure in God's Sight (Summary)
Here, then, is what we learn from James 1 about the person whose "religion" is superior to mere participation in church ceremonies and forms:

1. He recognizes that God is the source of every gift or endowment.

2. He knows that we can depend on God's unchanging love and power.

3. He acknowledges God as the source of spiritual life.

4. He exercises self-control, especially of his tongue and temper.

5. He puts aside all that displeases God, and receives God's Word with humility of spirit.

6. He wants to *obey* the Bible rather than merely to *learn* about it.

7. He is helpful to all—especially the helpless—who are in need.

8. He keeps himself unstained by the world around him.

Think and Do
Check yourself by the "Summary" above. Which items represent a definite need or weakness on your part? Do you tend to follow the world's ways of thinking? Are you expressing your love for God in loving service to those who need you? Are you studying the Bible systematically and intelligently?

What can you do, with God's help, to improve in one or more of these areas? Precisely what *will* you do? When will you start?

UNIT **4**

LOVE AND PARTIALITY

James 2:1-13

"My brethren, do not hold your faith in our glorious Lord Jesus Christ with an attitude of personal favoritism" (James 2:1).

Did you ever have a classmate who was "teacher's pet"? Have you worked in an office where someone who had an "in" with the boss took life easy while others worked hard? Or know a parent who favors one of his children?

Why is it that people are so often inclined to show partiality? (33)

In James 2 we read how partiality reveals itself (vv. 1-4). We also learn that sometimes God has chosen the very people others despise (vv. 5-7); that playing favorites is a sin (vv. 8-11); and that believers are to live under the law of liberty (vv. 12-13), which will enable them to overcome partiality.

If all Christians would live by the truths taught in James 2:1-13, our churches would be dramatically changed—for the better—almost overnight.

One Way of Being Partial in Church Relationships (James 2:1-4)
James gives us only one illustration of partiality, but the principle involved enters into all kinds of human relationships. The scene is the assembly of early Christians for worship. A man enters

whose fine robes and elegant gold ring mark him as obviously well-to-do. Another arrival's callous hands and worn clothing show that he is a poorly paid day-laborer.

An alert usher makes his way quickly to the rich man's side. "Right this way, please, sir," he whispers unctuously, showing the wealthy worshiper to the best seat available. "I hope you'll be comfortable here," he fawns. Then he goes back to the door and beckons the second man impatiently. "This way!" he snaps, seating him near a drafty window.

People who show this kind of partiality are "making class distinctions" (PH). They are "judges with evil motives" (v. 4). Their wrong motives and actions grow out of wrong attitudes.

"An attitude of personal favoritism" (v. 1) often shows that the person who has it is able to like only people who impress him favorably or who serve his personal interests. Such "small-ness" is as out of place in those who profess faith in "the Lord of glory" (v. 1, KJV) as it would be for members of a royal family to spend time looking at the peep shows in a penny arcade.

Stop and think about the situation in the church *you* attend. Is *everyone* who comes sure of a genuine welcome? If not, what kind of people might be made to feel they were somewhat less than *wanted* at the service?
(34)

What attitudes or actions on the part of the congregation would make it clear to these people that they were not wanted?
(35)

There are, happily, many churches—of almost all denominations —where a genuine and sincere welcome is extended to all. There are other churches that aim to attract only people of certain social, economic, or cultural levels. The members of these churches simply do not want to mingle with people of other nationalities, those with low incomes, people whose appearance or actions betray a lack of sophistication or "culture," or those who are without poise, charm, and style.

A national opinion poll reports that some Protestant denominations appeal primarily to wealthy, socially minded people. Others appeal to people in humbler circumstances. A formal liturgical church is at one end of the list, its membership heavy with socialites, political leaders, and executives. At the other end is a denomination noted for informality and emotionalism, with most of its members near the bottom of the economic totem pole.

Once in a while we read about "undesirables" being kept out of a church service by physical force, but most churches use the "cold shoulder" treatment. People do not necessarily do anything *insulting* toward an unwanted person—they just don't do *anything*. They simply ignore him, or look the other way if they think he may speak to them. They may even shake his hand impersonally, congratulating themselves on having done their unpleasant Christian duty. After enduring this treatment over a shorter or longer period, most men and women will break down and go to church elsewhere.

The people to whom we show partiality, or favoritism, are likely to be those in the "right" social and economic (or even political) group—those who come from the "right" families, nationalities, denominations, and what-not. But people in low-income brackets can be just as partial as middle-class folk. Those who are in the local minority—whether they be rich or poor—are most often discriminated against.

Why do you think partiality displeases the Lord?
(36)

Some human parents play favorites among their children, but "there is no partiality with God" (Rom. 2:11). All people, whether Christians or not, are His creatures. Christ died for *all*, and all who believe on Him become God's children and are on an equal basis before Him. "My brethren" (v. 1), the opening words of our chapter, remind us of our membership in God's family. God treats all His children alike.

But if a person who visits or attends your church is *not* a follower of Christ, why is it unthinkable that the church folk make him uncomfortable?

(37)

Such a person needs to find Christ. If you display lack of love, you make it unlikely that he will give the Gospel a fair hearing. By your snobbish attitude—because you don't like the cut of his clothes, his mannerisms, or some other trivial detail—you prejudice him against the Lord and the Gospel.

Partiality rears its ugly head in other ways, too, even in a Christian church. A Sunday School teacher or youth sponsor may play favorites. Sometimes he loses to the church, or even to the Lord, those whom his partiality alienates. In most churches there is an "in" group, usually a minority made up of the "leading" members of the congregation, who may limit their social contacts and personal friendships to other members of their select circle. They ignore members of the congregation whom they have not accepted into their choice clique. Those who are excluded by them may feel unwanted in the church. They may try to find acceptance elsewhere, perhaps at great spiritual compromise.

What are some of the ways you can show practical Christian love to those who visit or attend your church but do not feel they are genuinely wanted?

(38)

It takes more than a handshake from someone wearing a carnation in his buttonhole to make a person feel at home in a church. Your unofficial greetings, given with a friendly smile, will help. It's a good plan to introduce newcomers to as many other people as possible. Show a warm interest in them—without being inquisitive. Let them feel you are concerned for their problems in settling in the community, in facing family illness, etc. Invite newcomers to visit your home—or at least make a spontaneous friendly call in *their* homes, stopping in to inquire and to express interest. Invite them to go with you to church affairs. Cultivate genuine Christian concern for *everyone*—especially for those who are in minority groups or who seem to be generally ignored. This, of course, involves an expenditure of time and effort, and it is too "costly" for some Christians.

God's Apparent Choice of Poor People (James 2:5-7)

What qualities in other people lead you to want them for your friends?

(39)

A casual reading of verses 5-7 would give you the impression that poor people come off better than rich people in their dealings with God, but "there is no partiality with God" (Rom. 2:11). Wealth gives no one an advantage, but neither does poverty. Look closely at what James says here:

1. *Most Christians are not wealthy.* (This is not surprising, for most people in general, even in affluent America, are not rich.)

2. *The Gospel appeals more strongly to the poor than to the rich.* (Perhaps wealth tends to make a person feel he can get along without God.)

3. *Material poverty is no obstacle to the possession of real spiritual wealth.* (Many people who are poor in material goods are rich in the eternal things that really matter.)

The Gospel seems to be more popular among people who are not wealthy. Though there are many exceptions, it seems that as a class the "have nots" are more open to the Good News than the "haves." But most poor people, too, are unbelievers. Christians are a minority in almost any group.

Some rich people (v. 6) were oppressing the early Christians, dragging the believers into litigation and openly deriding the name of the Lord. This is not an indictment of *all* wealthy people—these particular men were not oppressors and blasphemers because they had lots of money, but because they had wicked hearts. Their money gave them power to do evil things, but they were no worse than wicked people whose poverty keeps them from indulging their wickedness. Tom, who commits a crime, is not much worse than Dick, who would have joined him had he been able to get out of jail!

Abraham Lincoln said that God must love common people because He made so many of them. The Lord loves poor people, too. God's message for the poor is that if they will set their love on Him (v. 5), they may become heirs of His kingdom. He will make them "rich in faith." This is true wealth that cannot fade away and is reserved in heaven for those to whom it belongs. It is available to the rich on exactly the same terms as to the poor.

God loves the poor and accepts them as readily as He accepts the rich, but some Christians were dishonoring the poor (v. 6) and favoring the rich.

Partiality—a Sin against the Royal Law (James 2:8-11)

James was ready to admit that perhaps the respect of some Christians for rich men in the church was prompted by genuine love. After all, rich people need as much love as poor folk, and sometimes they find it harder to get. Rich men often feel that what attracts others to them is their wealth; they view with suspicion every show of interest or expression of concern from one who has less money than they. These suspicious rich people need the healing therapy of Christian love, and so James says, in effect, "If you are treating rich men respectfully because you want to show them true Christian love, then you are doing well (cf. v. 8) and my rebuke does not apply to you."

(Incidentally, have you ever heard someone grumble because

the people in administrative positions in a church are often well-to-do? These leaders have usually been chosen for church positions because of the very traits that made them wealthy—leadership ability, good business sense, and sound judgment.)

Love is called "the royal law." It sums up all our responsibilities to our fellow men: "You shall love your neighbor as yourself" (v. 8; cf. Lev. 19:18; Mark 12:28-33; Rom. 13:8-10; Gal. 5:14). "He who loves his neighbor has fulfilled the Law" (Rom. 13:8).

But what is love? Christian love is a good deal more than a sentimental feeling. It is not gauged by what we *say,* or even by how we *feel,* but—as we saw in our last study—by what we *do.* What, in our attitude, will make others aware of our loving concern for them?

(40)

This world is full of people—and so is your community, and perhaps your church—who suffer keenly because they are not accepted. They are not hated, but they have a gnawing feeling that somehow they don't matter to others, or don't "fit in." Sometimes such people, because of our neglect, move to another church; sometimes they become terribly ingrown and feel more and more shut out of Christian fellowship. Sometimes, in "retaliation," they adopt unacceptable standards of conduct and become spiritual casualties.

These people, whom we often treat like the "poor" man of James 2, need nothing so much as they need love. They need to feel that you accept them as they are. Christ loved people as they were, and He still does. He wants people to feel His love through Christians, in whom He lives. Do you find it hard to love some people? Remember that God loves them, that if you are a Christian God indwells you, and that God wants to use you—your hands, your words, your affection—to touch, with a glow of new hope, the lives of those who desperately need love:

the poor, the stranger, the unsuccessful, the unattractive.

Partiality is love's opposite. It goes out to those who are attractive, easy to like, able to do things for us. Christian love should include *these* people, too, but must not overlook those less attractive who need help.

Our responsibility to love without favoritism can pose problems for which there are no "easy" solutions. For instance, all of us tend to have our own circle of friends—people who for one reason or another are "special" to us. Kim and Kippy Damon are examples. This young couple have grown up in First Church, a rapidly expanding suburban congregation in a neighborhood that from a "social" standpoint is going downhill. The Damons teach Sunday School classes and Kim is on the board of trustees. They have a good income, a comfortable home, and as many friends as they can readily keep up with.

One Sunday Dr. Peters, pastor of First Church, preached a powerful sermon on "Love and Partiality." He stressed that people need acceptance and love. He pointed out that a number of families—perhaps because they had not felt wanted—had not remained at First Church. He asked his congregation to open their hearts and their homes to those newcomers who were not making social contacts that would link them more strongly to Christianity.

The Damons felt convicted. They went to see Dr. Peters and told him they wanted to help, but said they already had all the social life they had time for. What should they do? Should they drop some of their old friends to make room for new ones? Should they entertain people with whom they had little in common or who didn't appeal to them? Wouldn't that be hypocritical?

If you were Dr. Peters, what would you say to Kim and Kippy Damon?

(41)

Having people in one's home regularly—even for the simplest and easiest kind of entertaining—is not the only way of expressing Christian love. In fact, people of diverse economic, social, or national backgrounds are not always happy to mingle together socially. James puts the emphasis where it belongs—on the church (vv. 2-4). One way of showing genuine love is by taking a sincere interest in people at church gatherings, by befriending them at socials, and by giving them opportunities to serve the church in various capacities instead of rotating the jobs among the "in" group. There is nothing wrong with a Christian's being intimate with a few people—unless this intimacy shuts out those whom God wants to love through him. Remember that partiality is not treated in this epistle as a weakness, or as an attitude somewhat less than desirable. It is plainly labeled (v. 9) as a sin. God warns that it is not to be trifled with. From man's point of view, partiality may make you seem superior, but in God's sight it makes you a lawbreaker (v. 10).

A pianist who strikes one wrong note produces a discord. A shirt soiled in one place is a dirty shirt. The Law is made of ten commandments. If we break a single one, we have broken the Law and are "guilty of all" (v. 10). This doesn't mean we are as guilty as if we had broken *all* the commandments; it means we are guilty of violating the Law.

Verse 11 cites two of the most glaring violations of the Law—adultery and murder. *All* the commands of the Law were given by God, and each of them is part of His total will. To break any one of them, then, is to act contrary to His will. To show partiality to certain people at the expense of fairness to others is to lack love. Love is the first and great commandment. Lack of love, therefore, makes us lawbreakers.

Liberty and Mercy (James 2:12-13)

You are to live as is fitting to one who is under the "law of liberty"—the principle of freedom by which Christians are to be governed. If you are a Christian, you are not under the law of commandments—the "Thou shalt nots." You are not required to live under restrictive regulations. God has put His Spirit within you and if you will allow Him to, the Spirit will make you *want* to obey God's will. *This* is the law, or principle, of liberty.

The ideal Christian life is not a matter of coercion and restraint; "I've *got* to read my Bible" or "I *mustn't* do this or that." If you have made a total commitment to Christ, the indwelling Holy Spirit will sooner or later give you an instinctive inclination to love God and others and to do what pleases the Lord. This law of liberty will prompt you to love *all* men rather than to give yourself only to a favorite few.

Mercy (v. 13) is a way in which love expresses itself. Your love and mercy can't possibly earn you God's forgiveness. One who shows no mercy, however, may reveal by his hardness of heart that he is not a partaker of God's nature through the new birth. He does not belong to God's family, and so has no share in the forgiveness which God offers freely to those who come to Him through faith in Christ (cf. Eph. 2:8-9). And if a person who lacks mercy is truly a Christian, he may expect that others will have no mercy on *him* when *he* is overtaken in a fault.

Love and Partiality (Summary)

Let's review what we have learned in James 2:

1. Those who believe in Christ are not to show partiality.

2. Men—even Christians—are inclined to judge people by appearances, income, nationality, social position, and other external factors.

3. Partiality influences our treatment of others, even in church.

4. As a result, some people turn from the Church and the Gospel because they feel unwanted.

5. Partiality violates the royal law of love, for we do not show love toward those against whom we discriminate.

6. Partiality is ungodlike, for with God there is no respect of persons. His love and grace go out equally to all kinds of people.

7. Those who are partial violate the will of God and are lawbreakers.

Think and Do

Why do *you* discriminate against people? Against fellow Christians? In what ways do you show favoritism or partiality? How do you show partiality in your home? On your job? In your church?

If you are a Christian, are you ready to yield your will to God's love, of which He wants to make others conscious through you? Will you *now* ask the Lord to help you rid your heart of the pride, bitterness, indifference, or selfishness that usually are at the root of unloving (and unlovely) partiality, in the pressure of which the good life is impossible?

FAITH AND GOOD WORKS

James 2:14-26

*"For just as the body without the spirit is dead,
so also faith without works is dead"* (James 2:26).

Alan Abbott and Bill Babbitt and their wives are in their twenties. Both couples profess to be Christians and both are moral, respectable people.

The Abbotts are active church members. They teach Sunday School classes, attend Sunday morning and evening services, go to prayer meetings regularly, have family devotions, and are tithers. They also give generously to various secular causes— welfare funds, the cancer drive, Christmas seals, and the like. Their home is open to visiting church speakers, missionaries, and others who need a night's lodging. They frequently discuss spiritual matters with friends and acquaintances, and they witness to strangers when occasion arises.

The Babbitts usually take their children to Sunday School. They go to church occasionally themselves, though their church membership is still back in the town where they grew up. They do not have family or personal devotions. Their income is larger than the Abbotts', but they budget only $50 a year for "church and charity." They never discuss their "religion." However, they know the facts of the Gospel. If you were to press them, they would tell you that a person is saved by grace through faith, and not by good works.

Why would it be wrong to say that the Abbotts are *undoubtedly* Christians and that the Babbitts cannot *possibly* be saved?

(42)

Let's study James 2:14-26 with the Abbotts and the Babbitts in mind. It would be well, before going further, to read the entire passage carefully. It is important to study it as a whole, getting its general content in mind, before looking at it more closely.

No Conflict on How We Are Saved (James 2:14-15)

The latter half of James 2 is usually regarded as a controversial passage because it *seems* hard to reconcile it with other plain statements of Scripture about salvation. Martin Luther, for all his capable exposition of the Bible, was inclined to classify James as "an epistle of straw" because it seemed to contradict his favorite doctrine, salvation by grace through faith apart from works. Study these three statements:

1. James says plainly that faith without works is dead, or barren (vv. 17, 20, 26). Some take this to imply that works (or good deeds) are necessary to salvation (cf. vv. 22, 24). Elsewhere (cf. Eph. 2:8-10) we read that we are saved by grace through faith, and *not* by works.

2. James says plainly that Abraham was justified by his works (vv. 21-23). Elsewhere (e.g., Rom. 4:1-12) we read that Abraham was justified by his faith, not by works.

3. James lists Rahab as another example of justification by works (James 2:25). Elsewhere (Heb. 11:31), we read that Rahab was saved by her faith.

It is true that the Bible contains statements, similar to those we have just mentioned, that *appear* to be contradictory. Some people, in the face of this fact, conclude that one or both the "contradictory" statements *must* be wrong. Other people try to understand and explain the two "conflicting" statements in a way that will be fair to both. Bible critics often take the first approach; Bible scholars usually take the second.

Let's try the second approach to the apparent contradictions between James 2 and the rest of Scripture. First, re-read carefully James 2:14-26; Ephesians 2:8-10; Romans 4:1-12; and Hebrews 11:31.

Does James 2 anywhere state plainly that we are *not* saved by faith?

(43)

Does James 2 anywhere state plainly that we are *saved* by works?

(44)

Do other passages say that faith is not to be accompanied by works?

(45)

You can see that the "contradiction" is not as strong as it may at first have seemed to be. James implies plainly that we are not saved by the kind of faith that doesn't produce good works, but he makes it clear that salvation *is by faith,* or by believing (James 2:23). The other passages also say that faith, *not* good works, is responsible for salvation—but they add that God wants good works to follow our being saved (Eph. 2:10).

But that is not all. Many words have two or more meanings. For instance, when a little girl sees the word *bow,* she probably thinks of a hair ribbon. But when a sailor sees the word *bow,* he may think of the front part of a ship. To a fireman, *hose* suggests a rubber tube; but *hose* makes the average woman think of her nylons. There are hundreds of words that have two, three, or a dozen meanings, as a glance into an unabridged dictionary will convince you.

For this reason, two people cannot communicate effectively

unless both the person who talks (or writes) and the person who listens (or reads) attach the same meanings to the words that pass between them. This is especially true when words have to do with ideas and abstractions rather than with tangible *things*. Ideas are slippery and elusive at best!

"Faith" and "justified" are technical theological terms. They, too, have more than a single meaning each. We must ask ourselves, then, whether all New Testament writers use these terms in the same way. Study these definitions:

	First Definition	*Second Definition*
FAITH	Belief that something is true	Personal trust, or commitment, to a person or truth
JUSTIFY	To declare righteous or just; to free from guilt (something God does)	To vindicate oneself or prove oneself righteous (something a man does)

A person with the first kind of faith admits that the Gospel is true—and stops there. A person with the second kind of faith says, "Because I believe the Gospel is true, I commit myself fully to Christ and trust Him for my personal salvation."

The word "justify," in the first sense, tells what God does for a person who trusts Christ as his sin bearer. Because Christ died for a believer's sins, God declares such a believer righteous, or just (justified). The second sense of the word expresses what a person does about his own faith in the eyes of other people—he justifies (or vindicates) himself—he proves by his actions that God has made him righteous.

From your study of James 2, check the meanings with which you think the writer of this epistle used each of these two terms: (46)

FAITH ( ) Mere belief ( ) Personal commitment
JUSTIFY ( ) To declare ( ) To prove oneself
righteous righteous

What meanings do you think were intended by the writers of

the other New Testament passages we have referred to?
(47)

FAITH	( ) Mere belief	( ) Personal commitment
JUSTIFY	( ) To declare righteous	( ) To prove oneself righteous

In view of the different meanings James and the other writers attach to the terms they use, and because James does not deny salvation by faith nor the others deny the importance of good works, you can readily see that there is no real conflict between James 2 and the rest of the New Testament.

Now let's look more closely at our James 2 passage.

The Kind of "Faith" That Is Dead (James 2:16-17)

Christian faith is to be accompanied by good deeds, or good works. List eight or ten examples of such good deeds:
(48)

Do not limit your thinking about "good deeds" to such "spiritual" activities as praying, reading the Bible, meditating, testifying, preaching, going to church, teaching Sunday School, and the like. These are all good works—but so are such ordinary, down-to-earth acts as visiting a sick person, paying your bills, telling the truth, controlling your temper, and being consistently kind and helpful (e.g., baby-sitting so that a neighbor can visit her husband in the hospital). Good works are simple, practical out-workings of Christian love. They are things you do for other people, including the poor (vv. 16-17), because of your love for Christ. Good deeds are Christian love in action.

Being a Christian, or being "saved," as we have previously pointed out, is not merely a matter of believing certain things to be true—though being a Christian *starts* with such belief. (That's why Christians have always been called "believers.") Being a Christian is primarily a relationship between a person and God. A person who trusts Christ as his personal Sin-bearer becomes, through that trust, a member of God's family. The Holy Spirit—the Spirit of Truth, goodness, power, light, and joy —comes to live in such a person's heart. The Spirit's presence there inclines the believer to good works—not in order that he may *be* saved, but because he *has been* saved and now *wants* to do the will of God, which includes right living and loving concern for others.

In other words, when Christ (or God, or the Holy Spirit—the Three are One) lives in you, He will make you *want* to do what otherwise you might merely feel you *ought* or *had* to do. The difference between *want to* and *ought to* is one difference between a Christian and a merely religious person. A Christian engages in good deeds because he delights in pleasing God. A religious person does good works because he thinks he ought to or because he thinks that in so doing he can earn acceptance with God.

Tom thinks the boss may "tap" him for the company team that will be sent on a tour of Europe next summer. He is working as hard as possible, hoping that his show of ambition will impress Mr. Big favorably and result in his being chosen. Harry is already on the team. He, too, is working hard—not to keep his place on the team but because he is "sold" on his company's product and has committed himself to the company's welfare. Tom is like a religious person, who thinks his good life will *earn* him salvation. Harry is like a Christian, whose good works are an *outgrowth* of his salvation.

Faith With and Without Good Deeds (James 2:18-20)
Restate in your own words the wrong thinking that James sets out to correct in the latter part of James 2:
(49)

It is entirely correct, then, to say that salvation is to be had only through faith, and that good deeds have nothing to do with one's becoming a Christian, a member of God's family. Unfortunately, some people, like the Bill Babbitts (p. 55), abuse this fact. They think that since salvation is all of faith, a Christian's conduct does not matter and he may do as he pleases. As long as one "believes" the right doctrines, they say, he is sure of heaven.

But James says, "Show me your faith without the works, and I will show you my faith by my works" (v. 18). This is really sarcasm. How *can* a person show his faith apart from what he *is* and *does?* Merely *saying* that one has faith is quite unconvincing. One's deeds must confirm his words. Good deeds, if not performed in an effort to earn salvation, can be valid evidence of genuine faith.

Sometimes a person's "faith" is merely intellectual belief. It may consist, for example, only in his believing the facts of the Gospel record—that Christ died for sinners and rose again, etc. Such "faith" is not likely to have much effect on how its owner *acts.* It is like the belief in careful driving that most automobile drivers have. In spite of their belief in careful driving, people are involved in automobile accidents because of their carelessness on the road. But a motorist who has been threatened with loss of liability insurance or revocation of his driving license because of his carelessness will believe in careful driving in quite a different way. *His* belief will lead him to a very conscious attempt to exercise extreme caution whenever he is behind the wheel of his car.

Why, then, does not the belief of the demons (v. 19) save them? (50)

You may be sure that Satan and the demons know *and believe* the facts of the Gospel. They know the "plan of salvation," but they also know they will not escape judgment. Why not? Because they merely *acknowledge* God's truth. They are eternally lost because there is no element of personal trust in their "belief."

They have never *responded* to the truth.

It is by what people *say* they are, and by how they *live*, that we must decide whether they need evangelizing or have already responded to the Gospel. For the most part, however, measure *other people* by their profession and measure *yourself* by your life. God will judge hypocrites in due season. Ask yourself whether *your* attitudes and actions indicate that God is living in you. If they don't, what ought you to do about the situation? (51)

You know about the girl who said she'd marry her fellow only "when apples grow on the lilac tree." Early in the morning the persistent chap was out tying apples onto the lilac bushes to meet her condition. Good deeds, however, are not apples to be tied to a lilac tree. Absence of good works may indicate either of two conditions, and you must decide which one applies to you:

1. You are a backslider—a Christian out of fellowship with God. If so, confess and forsake the sin that has come between you and the Lord.

2. You are not truly saved and lack vital faith, regardless of what you *say* about yourself. In that case, receive Christ as your Saviour.

The good works God wants will come *naturally*, not by self-effort, when your relationship to God is what it should be.

An old and apocryphal story tells about two preachers who were being rowed across a river. They discussed the relative importance of faith and works. When the boatman saw that the two "reverends" could not reconcile their views, he undertook—with the aplomb of a modern taxi driver—to settle the dispute. He said, "It's like this, gentlemen. The oar in my right hand is faith; the oar in my left hand is works. If I pull only on the oar of faith, you see the boat goes around in circles. If use only the oar of works, we go in circles, too—in the opposite direction. But when I pull on *both* oars, you see we go straight toward our destination. So, gentlemen, it is not faith without works, nor works without faith, but, as James said, faith *and* works."

What do you think is wrong with the boatman's explanation? (52)

For one thing, we are not going to heaven in a rowboat pulled by two oars! For another, James does *not* say we are saved by works without faith, but neither does he tell us we are saved by faith *plus works*. What he says is that the kind of faith that saves is the kind that produces good works. God saves us so that we may live a life of good works (Eph. 2:10). He equips us, by giving us His Holy Spirit, for this sort of life (cf. Phil. 2:14). If we fail to produce the good works that are to accompany faith, we are to examine ourselves carefully (2 Cor. 13:5) to make sure we have genuine faith rather than the kind which James so roundly condemns as "useless" and "dead." But it is *always* the faith, not the works, that saves us. Works are important as *evidence* of faith, but they have *no saving value whatever.*

Old Testament Examples of Living Faith (James 2:21-26)

The episode from Abraham's life to which James refers is recorded in Genesis 22. Abraham obeyed God's command that he sacrifice his only son, whom God had declared should be his heir, on a mountaintop altar. Critics object to this story as portraying a primitive, barbaric concept of God. They fail to notice that God did not actually *allow* Abraham to make the sacrifice. Why, then, do you think God told Abraham to sacrifice Isaac in the first place? (53)

God was not testing Abraham's faith, for He knew in advance what Abraham would do. Perhaps God wanted Abraham to grow in faith. He knew Abraham's trust would be "perfected" (v. 22) through this trying experience, and that he would become increasingly aware of the greatness of his love for God. Abraham's complete willingness to obey was positive proof to him *and to others* (including us) that his faith was no mere mental assent to a doctrinal statement, no mere verbal profession. His works justified, or vindicated, him (v. 21)—but *only because they were prompted by faith* (v. 22). The works added nothing to the saving value of his faith, but were its outworking in life. James goes on to state plainly that "*it* [Abraham's believing God] was reckoned to him as righteousness" (v. 23).

There are any number of people who are kind, generous, and good, or who are even religious, but who do not even *profess* to have faith in Jesus Christ. Some would insist that such people, no matter what their beliefs or lack of them, are acceptable to God. *This is not true.* Good works *must* be accompanied by genuine faith (v. 18). When people profess faith in God and combine their profession with consistently exemplary lives, they must be either genuine believers or consummate hypocrites, and it is not difficult to distinguish between these two extremes.

Rahab is the second Old Testament illustration of faith. She believed on the Lord God of Israel—and she showed her faith by helping the Israelite spies (Heb. 11:31; Josh. 2). Her actions, or works, justified her in the eyes of men and demonstrated that her faith was no mere verbal profession. Hers was the sort of faith that is the rock foundation of "the good life."

Saving Faith Is Working Faith (Summary)

Now for a quick look back over the second part of James 2 for the principal teachings of the passage:

1. One way in which faith expresses itself is in acts of loving helpfulness to those in need.

2. The kind of "faith" that is unaccompanied by good works is useless and dead; it has no saving value.

3. Good works done out of love for Christ are evidence of saving faith.

4. "Faith" without a personal commitment and trust is mere intellectual assent or verbal profession and is of no value in God's sight.

5. God justifies true believers because of their faith, but their works justify (vindicate) them in the eyes of men.

6. Genuine "good" works are not done to earn or "display" our salvation but as acts of gratitude to the One who saved us and gave us His good life.

Think and Do

Have you been trying to become a Christian by doing good deeds or by being religious? Can you see, now, the futility of this approach to the good life?

Is your faith a form of "only-believism"? Do you think that if you believe the right things are true, how you live makes no difference? Can you see how futile this attitude is?

What changes in your thinking will you ask the Lord to help you make? If you have not previously exercised saving faith, will you trust Christ now? If you *are* a Christian, in what good deeds will you put your faith to work?

CHRISTIANS AND SPEECH

James 3:1-12

*"No one can tame the tongue; it is a restless evil
and full of deadly poison"* (James 3:8).

Marvin, a young man of some promise, had come to town to be
interviewed for an important position with the Bogg Corporation.
He had been invited to dinner, along with a guest of his own
choosing, at the home of Mr. Bogg, president of the company.
Marvin discussed his opportunity with a pastor to whom a friend
back home had directed him, and the understanding pastor
offered to get him a suitable "date" for the occasion. Marvin
declined the offer and invited Carol, a strikingly beautiful girl
with whom he was acquainted only because she worked in the
cashier's cage at the hotel where he was staying.

Proud of the woman he was escorting, and certain that having
her with him would enhance the impression he made, Marvin
went confidently to the dinner party. As soon as Mr. Bogg tried
to begin a conversation with Carol, however, Marvin realized his
mistake. His beautiful "date" showed a woeful lack of culture,
and Marvin was relieved when the conversation by-passed her.
Near the end of the meal, however, Mr. Bogg asked Carol if
she would have another portion of dessert. "No, thanks," she
said brightly, pushing her plate back inelegantly and making a
crude but expressive gesture: "I'm full right up to my kiss-hole."

Appearances are deceiving, and it is often difficult or impossible to judge a person's character by how he looks. Usually,
however, the truth about him is out as soon as he begins to talk.

His pronunciation, use of words, and tone of voice enable us to judge fairly accurately his education, his degree of refinement, and his disposition or character. A person who speaks well, chooses his words with care, and modulates his voice pleasantly, is likely to be superior to the individual who is careless with his language, has a limited vocabulary, and speaks in a loud, strident voice. And since language is an expression of a man's thoughts, it may well reveal whether he is self-centered or is yielded to the control of the Lord Jesus Christ. A person who thinks himself to be religious, but does not bridle his tongue, deceives himself and has no "religion" that is worthwhile (cf. 1:26).

In chapter 3, James reverts to the important and interesting subject of speech and deals with it at length. He tells you that if you misuse the gift of speech you are heading for judgment (vv. 1-2); that your tongue's influence is out of all proportion to its size (vv. 3-5); that it will be difficult for you to control your tongue (vv. 6-8); and that you may use the gift of speech either for evil or for good (vv. 9-12).

Misuse of the Tongue Leads to Judgment (James 3:1-2)
Why is it true that a man who can control his tongue can usually control himself in other ways, too (v. 2b)—that is, for example, he can probably control his appetite, his actions, and his thoughts?
(54)

Most people will think twice before they commit an *act* that is definitely wrong—but many people will *speak* without thinking of the consequences. And the tongue (that is, the way we use the tongue) is so unruly and evil (v. 8) that for us to control it is practically impossible. Therefore, because it is so hard to control the tongue, a person who can do so probably can control himself in every other way. Ability to do the greater includes ability to do the lesser. A man who can lift 50 pounds can certainly lift 25 pounds. A person who can control what he *says* will be able to control what he *does*. In fact, he is likely to be a "perfect" man (v. 2)—one who is fully instructed, well balanced, and spiritually mature.

Some Bible scholars tell us that "the whole body" (v. 2) may be a reference to the Church, the body of Christ, which is made up of all regenerate individuals regardless of their denominational affiliations. If one accepts this interpretation, then the apostle is saying here that ability to control the tongue qualifies a person for a position of leadership or responsibility in the Church. You probably know of otherwise capable individuals who are disqualified for church office because of their uncontrolled tongues.

This view ties in with the warning with which the chapter begins: "Do not crowd in to be teachers" (Moffatt). There must have been, among the Christians to whom James wrote, much eagerness to become teachers, regardless of whether or not one was properly prepared by training and experience. What are some of the reasons why unqualified people want to teach—for example, in a Sunday School class?

(55)

No one should become a teacher unless he feels called of God to this particular service. You may be sure the Lord will not call a person who is not, or refuses to become, properly equipped. Where a church lacks teachers, depend upon it that the shortage does not exist because God is not ready to call and prepare people. Rather, some people are not listening for His call. When God's teachers ignore His call, we find Sunday School classes taught by men and women who would do better singing in the choir, sewing for the missionaries, or caring for babies in the nursery.

James warns against pushing one's way into a teaching position for reasons of self-satisfaction or prestige. Some people find it pleasant to speak in public, whether or not they have anything worth saying. They enjoy being a center of attention in the church or Sunday School. They like to display their knowledge of Scripture, however limited it may be.

Such people ought to think twice about what they are doing, says James, because as teachers they "are going to be judged with a stricter judgment than other people" (v. 1, wms). What *teachers* say, because of their position, will influence people far more than what *other* people say. Teachers will be judged on the basis of this greater responsibility. Don't become a teacher, then, unless God definitely calls you—but be sure to listen for His call and respond if and when it comes.

The Tongue, though Small, Is Influential (James 3:3-5)

> It's hard to tell the depth of a well
> > By the length of the handle on the pump;
> You cannot gauge a camel's age
> > By the color of the hair on his hump.

So went a popular song of many years ago. The principle involved is that there is usually no correlation between such things as the length of a pump handle and the depth of the well. Nor is there necessarily any significant relationship between the size of an object and its importance. This principle is true, for example, of people. Napoleon, one of the most influential and important men in all history, was of such small stature that his men affectionately called him "the Little Corporal."

James gives some illustrations of small but important objects. The bit (v. 3) by which we control a horse is rather insignificant in comparison with the bulk of the horse's body, but by it we cause the animal to go wherever we want him to take us, and stop him when we get there. The rudder of a ship (v. 4) is small by contrast with the remainder of the vessel, but by it the steersman turns the craft and causes it to go in whatever direction he chooses.

A fire (v. 5) usually has a small beginning. Back in 1871, a cow being milked by a Mrs. O'Leary in a Chicago barn kicked over her lamp and set fire to the hay in the stall. Before the flames were controlled, they had destroyed 17,450 buildings, including the entire business district of that great city. More than 250 people were killed. A great forest, representing the growth of trees over hundreds of years, has often been entirely wiped out because a careless camper or hunter has discarded a tiny lighted match among dry leaves and has started a conflagration that rages for days and does untold damage.

The tongue, too, is small (v. 5a) in comparison with the rest of the human body. In your relationships with other people, however, nothing can compare in importance and in influence with your tongue.

In what ways do you think the tongue (that is, the gift of speech) is like a fire (cf. v. 6)?
(56)

Fire may be put to either good or bad use. We cook our food and warm our homes with it, and use it in many manufacturing and industrial processes. Our civilization would be impossible without fire. But on the other hand, fire is capable of doing tremendous damage, especially when it gets out of control. When a bonfire ignites a hayfield or a stand of dry evergreens, or when a gas furnace explodes and hurls flames through the basement of a home, fire may become a monster of destructive proportions.

The tongue "is as dangerous as any fire, with vast potentialities for evil. It can poison the whole body; it can make the whole of life a blazing hell" (v. 6, PH). Can you give a few specific examples of what may happen when people use the tongue, the gift of speech, carelessly or maliciously?
(57)

The sins of speech are many and varied. There is lying, for

example—speaking or acting in such a way as to give an impression that is not true. For instance, an apocryphal doctor who was fond of horseback riding named his horse "Consultation." Then, when patients called and wanted to see him at once, his nurse would say, "Sorry—the doctor is out on Consultation." Or a businessman, to avoid seeing people for one reason or another, will have his secretary tell visitors he is "out."

Then there is gossip, or passing on groundless rumors about a person, and slander, or maliciously circulating false reports. Shakespeare makes Polonius say, about the various ways of assassinating a person's character,

> Who steals my purse steals trash,
> But he who filches from me my good name
> Robs me of that which not enriches him
> And leaves me poor indeed.

Sad to say, some Christians persistently engage in gossip and enjoy nothing more than finding some "juicy morsel" to pass on—sometimes even on the pretext that they are "spiritually concerned" for their victim.

Profanity is a common sin today—both among the lowest classes of people and among those who consider themselves ultra-highly sophisticated. Profanity is an offense against God, against the second commandment, and against the sensitivities of any Christians within earshot. So is coarse, vulgar talk—cheap use of the "four-letter words" that many modern writers have gone to such great lengths to popularize by overworking them in their "realistic" portrayals of the contemporary scene. Language that would not have been tolerated a few years ago is now widely accepted as an accurate "artistic" portrayal of modern life and appears in books available on any newsstand.

Exaggeration and misrepresentation are forms of lying that some people mistakenly think are acceptable under certain circumstances. And most people insist that it is not wrong to tell a "white" lie.

It would be hard to tell how many homes have been sad dened, friendships broken, marriages ruined, reputations lost, and futures darkened by the misuse of the tongue. A word fitly spoken is like apples of gold in pictures of silver (Prov. 25:11), but abuse of the tongue has dashed more hopes and caused more pain than most of us can imagine. And no matter how you may regret them or try to "explain" them, you can never "unsay" the words you speak. As well try to unscramble an egg!

You may unconsciously think that your words are not serious as long as they do not lead you to commit wrong acts. This is not in line with the teachings of our Lord Jesus Himself. He points out that in the day of judgment you will render an account for every careless word you speak. "By your words," He said, "you shall be justified, and by your words you shall be condemned" (Matt. 12:36-37). This warning deserves to be taken seriously. Keep in mind what the Apostle Paul said: "With the heart man believes, resulting in righteousness; and *with the mouth* he confesses, resulting in salvation" (Rom. 10:10). How you use the gift of speech, then, is vitally important—to you, to those who hear you, and to God. Your use of the tongue reveals how you think and whether your life is God-centered or self-centered. Your use of the gift of speech may determine whether or not "the good life" can be yours: "He that will love life and see good days, let him refrain his tongue from evil, and his lips that they speak no guile" (1 Peter 3:10).

The Tongue is Controlled Only with Difficulty (James 3:6-8)

As he comes back to the theme of verse 2 (cf. 1:26)—the matter of controlling the tongue—James reminds us that "every species of beasts and birds, of reptiles and creatures of the sea, is tamed and has been tamed by the human race" (v. 7).

In her intriguing books, *Born Free, Living Free,* and *Forever Free,* Joy Adamson tells how she and her husband reared Elsa, a man-eating lioness. Many lions have been reared and tamed in captivity, but Elsa was perhaps the first one whose tamers did not have to choose, at the animal's maturity, between putting their pet in a zoo and releasing it to live in the forest without the ability, born of experience, to make its own way. The Adamsons had so trained Elsa that after they had released her to live in the forest, she not only survived but remained their friend and always greeted them affectionately on the frequent visits they made to her and her cubs.

Other beasts, less ferocious than lions, have also been tamed. Many kinds of birds have been men's pets. Even the fierce falcon, a fighting bird, will submit to being carried on the falconer's wrist. Men have made pets of venomous snakes. They have succeeded in training lizards and even alligators. A number of the creatures of the sea have been domesticated. In fact, enough species of animals have been trained (v. 7) to demonstrate that men are able to tame practically any creatures they choose to.

Man's ability to control that which is wild and ferocious by nature has been well established, but there is one wild beast, full of deadly poison, that men simply cannot control completely. That "beast" is the tongue—the power of human speech. The word "but," with which verse 8 begins, suggests a contrast between the wild animals of nature, which men have been able to bring under their dominion, and the wild, restless, and evil tongue. Writing by inspiration, James concludes that *"no one can tame the tongue."* This rather strikingly final statement is made without reservation or exception.

Now compare the fact that you are unable to control the tongue (v. 8) with verse 2 of this chapter. Since no man *can* control the tongue, how *does* anyone who wants to qualify as a teacher, or as a mature Christian, avoid sinning in the area of speech? (58)

Obviously, only the supernatural power of God can enable you to control the perverse and wayward tongue. That is why the extent to which you control your speech is an index to your yieldedness to God. The more a Christian is obeying the Holy Spirit, the greater will be his ability to control himself in every area of life—including how he uses his speech.

The Tongue Speaks Both Good and Evil (James 3:9-12)

We have already thought about some of the *bad* uses you may make of the power of speech. Try now to think of some of the *good* uses to which you may put the tongue—uses that will help others and serve God. List them here:

(59)

Presumably you have included in your list such instances of speech as preaching the Gospel, teaching, witnessing, comforting, encouraging, cheering, and the like. But have you included the expression of appreciation, the friendly giving of genuinely constructive criticism, and the putting into words of your feelings of love? One could make quite a list of the good functions of the power of speech. And isn't it remarkable that the same person may put the tongue to both good and bad uses? (v. 10) Most of us are painfully inconsistent in how we handle the gift of speech. At one moment we use it to praise and worship the Lord; a little while later we use it to berate fellowmen who are made in the image of the God we profess to worship (v. 9). Why do you think people are so inconsistent in the way they speak?

(60)

A fountain, James reminds us, doesn't send out both fresh and bitter water from the same opening (v. 11). A fig tree bears figs, not olives; a vine bears grapes, not figs (v. 12). If we fill a pitcher with salt water, we must expect salt water to come out of it when we pour. There is a consistency in nature that is sometimes missing in human beings!

This does not contradict the truth that how a person *usually* talks reveals what he is. Even a good person can misuse the gift of speech, as James has implied (vv. 2, 8)—and even a wicked person can occasionally—or quite often—say something good.

"These things ought not to be this way" (v. 10). Inconsistency is displeasing to God. Since it is His purpose that you always use your tongue to bless others and glorify Him, He is ready and able, through the gift of His Holy Spirit, to make it possible for you to do this (2 Cor. 9:8).

Christians and Speech (Summary)

Let's think back over the first part of James 3 and review the lessons the writer gives us here. What do you learn about the gift of speech.

1. Those who teach will be judged by standards more strict than those by which non-teachers are judged.

2. It follows that a person should not assume the position of teacher unless he has a definite call from God.

3. How a person controls his tongue is an index to his spiritual maturity.

4. The tongue has a power that is far out of proportion to its relatively small size.

5. The tongue, if it is used wrongly, can be as destructive as a fire in its effects.

6. It is impossible for a person, apart from the power of the Holy Spirit, to control his tongue completely.

7. Christians are often inconsistent. They sometimes use their tongues rightly, and sometimes wrongly.

Think and Do

What habits of speech does the Lord want *you* to eliminate from your life? Are you addicted to telling lies? To exaggeration? To hasty, thoughtless words? To gossip? To cruel, cutting remarks? To character assassination? To boasting?

What good habits of speech should you be cultivating? Do you encourage those who face problems? Do you find words of true appreciation to say about other people? Do you express, in words, your love or concern? Do you comfort those who are sorrowing?

What wrong habit of speech will you ask the Lord to help you eliminate this week? What right habit will you ask Him to help you cultivate? Ask Him now; begin today!

WISDOM AND HUMILITY

James 3:13—4:10

"Who among you is wise and understanding? Let him show by his good behavior his deeds in the gentleness of wisdom" (James 3:13).

A. A. Milne's celebrated Winnie-the-Pooh, by his own admission, was a bear of little brain. People who are similarly small in spiritual discernment think the two essential ingredients of the good life are money and health. They reason that if one is rich and healthy he is in a position to get and to enjoy whatever else is necessary.

Most people, however, are more discerning than the somewhat limited (if charming) Pooh. They will agree that if one is to enjoy the good things of life he *also* needs a certain amount of intelligence. And for the *truly* good life, which God wants all His people to have, James mentions two qualities that are absolutely indispensable—wisdom and humility. The two go hand in hand.

How about jotting down the differences you can think of between *knowledge* and *wisdom.* (You may want to use a dictionary!) (61)

We'll come back to that difference presently—but for now, read the entire passage (James 3:13—4:10). Then look back and notice the topics with which the apostle deals: a person's wisdom will show in what he does (3:13); counterfeit wisdom will produce disharmony (vv. 14-16), but wisdom from heaven brings peace (vv. 17-18); lack of wisdom results in discord (4:1-3) and worldliness (vv. 4-5); and the remedy for worldliness is humility (vv. 6-10).

True Wisdom Reflected in One's Conduct (James 3:13)

Sometimes we confuse knowledge and wisdom. Knowledge is the possession of facts, information, or skill acquired through training or experience. Wisdom is superior to knowledge—it is skill in the *use* of knowledge. It is keen insight and ability to judge soundly. A person with a good education may have knowledge, but if he lacks wisdom he will find it hard to make good use of the facts he has learned. On the other hand, a person who has wisdom will be shrewd and discerning even though he lacks formal education. Sometimes we say such a person "has what it takes."

As the term is used in the Bible, wisdom is based on respect for and personal trust in the Lord: "The fear of the Lord is the beginning of wisdom" (Prov. 9:10). Wisdom that does not include obedience to God's Word is spiritually useless. A "wise" man (v. 13), in God's sight, is not necessarily a person who has earned a graduate degree. He is a believer in Christ who lives in accordance with God's will. That is why James says, "Are there some wise and understanding men among you? Then [their] lives will be an example of the humility that is born of true wisdom" (v. 13, PH).

But if a person is truly wise, why will he be truly humble as well?

(62)

A wise man recognizes his relationship to God. He acknowledges God's greatness, holiness, and majesty. He is aware that in himself he cannot meet God's requirements for goodness and faithfulness—he is something like an untrained savage tribesman trying to operate an advanced model computer. His awareness of personal inability makes him humble before God, and his humility leads him to the sort of conduct God requires.

Counterfeit Wisdom Produces Lack of Humility (James 3:14-16)

God's wisdom, which He gives you for the asking (1:5), is not the only "wisdom" available, however. Satan has a spurious substitute product for almost everything God gives men. He even has his substitute for God's good life—it is seen in the happy, carefree attitudes of so many unbelievers. The devil has his brand of wisdom, too. It is "earthly" (v. 15)—it is the wisdom of this world (1 Cor. 1:20). A person limited to *this* wisdom cannot grasp God's truth (1 Cor. 2:14). Such wisdom is sensual, or "natural" (as opposed to spiritual). It is "demonic," in that it originates with Satan rather than with God. It leads to arrogance, smugness, superiority, self-sufficiency, abandonment of God's morality and authority, lack of truthfulness, selfish ambition, bitter jealousy, and humanistic philosophies contrary to God's Word (cf. vv. 14, 16).

What might a building contractor, for example, do in constructing a house "on speculation" if he were trying to "get ahead" financially by the exercise of this spurious wisdom? (63)

The devil's wisdom, or the world's wisdom—they often amount to the same thing—is to be seen all around us. As an illustration, this is the "wisdom" of the aggressive man who knows how to get what he wants, at the expense of all who stand in his way, without regard to the demands of personal integrity and without respect for God's moral law.

The contractor we mentioned could use shoddy materials where they wouldn't show. He could "skimp" on nails (and a year or two later all the floors in the house would squeak). He could use a lean mixture of cement in his concrete (and within a few years a driveway or a sidewalk would show pockmarks). He could lay a poor foundation, which would cause the house to sag in spots, making it difficult for the people in it to open and close windows. He could save perhaps $500 on each house he built—but it would cost the owner thousands of dollars to correct the resulting structural defects.

A family had waited in line for some time to see an exhibit at a county fair. Just as they got to the entrance, a boy of about 12 stepped into the line in front of them. The annoyed parents told the lad to go back to the end of the long line and wait his turn. He left, but was back in a minute or two with his father, a determined-looking man who pointedly said to his son in a loud voice, "Stand *here*! Just tell *me* if anyone has anything to say about it!" This father, with earthly wisdom, was giving his son a lesson in how to "get ahead" (literally!) without regard for convention or the rights of others.

"Disorder and every evil thing" follow in the wake of the wrong kind of "wisdom." People who are "smart" rather than wise really know little personally about genuine peace and the true goodness of life. They are often responsible for unhappiness and injustice among those whom they victimize.

Heavenly Wisdom Leads to Peace (James 3:17-18)

We have seen the qualities of the kind of wisdom that originates in the world and the flesh and is from the devil. Notice, by way of contrast, the qualities (v. 17) of the kind of wisdom God gives those who ask Him for it:

1. It is from God rather than from the devil.
2. It is pure—free from the defilement of fleshly thinking.
3. It is peaceable and avoids conflict and dissension.
4. It is gentle rather than harsh.
5. It is reasonable—ready to be conciliated and to "meet people halfway."
6. It is merciful, ready to take the initiative in forgiving.
7. It is fruitful in terms of right motives and conduct.
8. It is unwavering, available whenever it is needed.

9. It is sincere and genuine—"straightforward" (Moffatt); it does not pretend to be what it is not.

Phillips translates: "The wisdom that comes from God is first utterly pure, then peace-loving, gentle, approachable, full of tolerant thoughts and kindly actions, with no breath of favoritism or hint of hypocrisy."

If most Christians lived by this sort of wisdom, what are a few improvements that would take place in their contacts with one another and with the unchurched people they are trying to reach with the Gospel?

(64)

A person who is truly wise sows peace because he is a peacemaker (cf. v. 18).

Lack of Wisdom Leads to Discord (James 4:1-3)

Why do you think some Christians lack the qualities in the list above? Why is there so much discord and feuding among Christians?

(65)

Some people jump to the conclusion that the "fightings and wars" (KJV) mentioned here have to do with international conflicts, but notice that the discord of which James writes is "among *you*"—that is, among *Christians*. James may be talking about strife and contention among Christians over doctrinal issues. If so, the implication is that some Christians get a lot of satisfaction from proving that their opponents are wrong. A great deal of contending for the faith thoroughly lacks the spirit of love that is to distinguish everything a Christian does. The late G. Campbell Morgan wrote that when he heard of some Christians contending for sound doctrine he was more concerned for the spiritual condition of those who did the contending than for the people they accused of wrong theological views.

But doctrinal disputes are not the only source of quarrels and conflicts among God's people when, in their lack of wisdom, they allow themselves to be governed by "the desires which are ever at war within [their] bodies" (v. 1, WMS). Some believers, like infants, want what they want when they want it. They are slaves to their desires. What are some of the things of which Christians become so inordinately fond that they stop at nothing to get them? (66)

People who want something badly enough will even "commit murder" (v. 2) to get it. When they do not have the things for which they envy others, they fight and quarrel in order to get them, instead of asking God for them—or better, asking that they may be content with what they have. When they *do* ask God, they may fail to get what they ask because their motives in asking are wrong (v. 3)—they are interested only in what will satisfy their baser impulses. Or, they are utterly selfish in their praying. They want such things as popularity, friends, money, comfort, and the like, far more than they want spiritual maturity, discernment, and fruitfulness in God's service. They are satisfied with *good* things rather than longing for God's *best* gifts. They value temporal blessings above eternal blessings—an evidence of their lack of true wisdom.

Lack of Wisdom Leads to Worldliness (James 4:4-5)

From our previous definition of the world (as the term is used in the New Testament, cf. p. 42), define *worldliness*. (67)

A worldly person doesn't appreciate the reality and value of the spiritual. He is so preoccupied with this present life that he has little or no heart for spiritual development and for the worship and service of God.

Why do you think the world is so attractive to many Christians? (68)

Many elements of "the world," or man's realm of life, are pagan or immoral. Many others, however—for example, art, literature, and music—are in themselves neutral or capable of being used for good. But when even good things crowd God out or put Him in second place, they become evil.

The world appeals to the lust of the eyes, the lust of the flesh, and the pride of life. It appeals to human intelligence and pride. It is pleasing to "the flesh"—and, unfortunately, many Christians live "after the flesh." They feel that "the good life" demands that they conform to the fashions, customs, and habits of people around them who do not take God into account.

A married woman who divides her allegiance between two men is an adulteress. So is a Christian who divides his allegiance between God and the world. Such a Christian is like a "faithless wife" (v. 4, WMS), because lack of loyalty to God and Christ constitutes spiritual adultery.

Teenage city gangs would give short shrift to a youth who tried to belong to two rival gangs at the same time. Such a teen would find himself speedily rejected and punished by both sides. One can't at the same time be a "Black Tiger" and a "Green Hornet." Nor can one at the same time serve both God and mammon (Matt. 6:24). And to be the friend of the world is to be the enemy of God (James 4:4).

Williams translates verse 5: "Do you think that the Scripture means nothing when it says, He jealously yearns for the Spirit that He causes to dwell in your hearts?" God wants the Holy Spirit to have full control of your will. To divide your allegiance between Him and the world is spiritual adultery, a serious sin which some Christians are inclined to treat lightly.

A new Christian had been urged to speak the whole truth at all times. He told his wife, who had not yet come to Christ, that for 14 years he had been unfaithful to her. That night his wife killed herself. To know that a loved one has been untrue is more of a shock than some people can stand. A wife, an employer, the armed services—all *insist* on loyalty. So does God. It is the part of wisdom to shun worldliness as you would shun the plague. It is dangerous to try to see how worldly you can be and still be a Christian.

Humility—Secret of Victory over Worldliness (James 4:6-10)

We have seen that wisdom and humility are closely associated (v. 13). A truly wise person recognizes humility as the only acceptable attitude in the light of how his weakness and sinfulness contrast with God's omnipotence and holiness. Worldliness and pride are also related. To overcome the temptation to worldliness, one must depend not on himself but on God's grace. It is the humble person to whom God *gives* grace (v. 6) for this and for every other victory. Humble people, *because of* their humility, depend on God for grace—the ability to do what is right—and God does not disappoint them.

How does God show that He is "opposed to the proud"? (v. 6) (69)

Suppose you visited a friend and found him repairing a piece of furniture. Suppose you knew, from your past experience, that he was using the wrong kind of glue. You would probably tell him how to do the job properly, but if he refused to pay attention to you, you would no doubt allow him to go on in his own proud way and take the consequences. A spiritually proud man is one who is convinced he knows more or can do better by himself than with God's help. God is "opposed" to such a man. Sometimes God intervenes and acts to rebuke a proud man, but often

He "resists" (KJV) him by merely allowing him to go on in his folly and find out his mistake for himself. So it is much more sensible to "submit . . . to God" (v. 7) and do things *His* way. It is always the best way.

Notice the two commands that follow, in verses 7b, 8a. Just how would you go about resisting the devil?
(70)

How would you go about drawing near to God?
(71)

Have you ever felt the bitterness of wanting to be near a loved one who had no desire to be near you? The great heart of God yearns for nearness to His children. Drawing near to God, however, involves something more than merely praying. It calls for a deep, full surrender to Him—letting go of anything that comes between you and Him, a walking closely with Him, as Enoch walked (Gen. 5:22-24). If you draw near to God, you quit fighting His plan for you, you put yourself fully at His disposal, and you accept without question whatever He sends. You find your greatest joy in doing His will. Drawing near to God is the ultimate expression of the life of faith, of complete dependence on the Lord; it will result in God's drawing near to you in a richly satisfying spiritual experience.

Resisting the devil, on the other hand, means recognizing Satan's presence, intentions, and power—and refusing to yield to his temptings. When temptation comes, remember that *you do not have to give in* (1 Cor. 10:13).

You can't very well resist the devil and draw near to God without proper preparation (v. 8b). If there is sin on your hands, you need the cleansing of confession and forgiveness. If you are double-minded and not sure whether you are living for God or for the world, your heart must be purified and unified (Ps. 86:11c). With the help of the Holy Spirit, you must make up your mind, once for all, to give God His way. If you have failed God in the past, you need to feel the godly sorrow (v. 9) that leads to repentance (2 Cor. 7:10).

Above all, humble yourself before God and He will "lift you up." The people of James' day, when they wanted to express contrition, would roll in the dust until they were pardoned by the one whom they had offended. You needn't do that literally, but tell God sincerely that you need and want His pardon. He will forgive you and His grace will help you avoid worldliness and other sins.

Wisdom and Humility (Summary)

This is the longest of any of our studies in James. Let's review its teachings:

1. True spiritual wisdom is evident in a good life—and particularly in a person's humility about what he is and does.

2. Jealousy, inordinate personal ambition, arrogance, falsehood, and disorder are indications that one is living by the spurious "wisdom" that does not originate in God.

3. Such counterfeit wisdom comes from Satan and has nothing in common with heaven or with things that are spiritual.

4. God's wisdom makes a person pure-minded, easy to get along with, sincere, loving, and peaceable.

5. If you allow your desires to control you, you will fight selfishly for whatever you want.

6. You may fail to receive God's good gifts because you do not ask for them or because you ask out of selfish motives.

7. If you choose friendship with the world-system around you, you make yourself an enemy of God, who yearns to have you *wholly* His.

8. You need God's grace to overcome worldliness, and He gives it to those who are humble before Him.

9. In order to draw near to God you must repent and turn from sin and double-mindedness.

Think and Do

God draws His people toward Him—but the world and its charms pull them in the other direction. The nearer you are to God, the farther—spiritually speaking—you will be from the world. Does the world, with its materialistic values, still have first claim on your thinking? Do you have trouble keeping this life and eternity in proper perspective?

Humble yourself before God by admitting—to yourself and to Him—that you need Him desperately. Draw near to Him, and He will draw near to you. He will become so real to you that you will find yourself living by the value system of heaven rather than by that which prevails on earth.

TAKING GOD INTO ACCOUNT

James 4:11—5:6

"You do not know what your life will be like tomorrow. You are just a vapor that appears for a little while and then vanishes away" (James 4:14).

If Jesus Christ came to your community today, how do you think people would respond to His message? (72)

Thinking about the effects on people of such an imaginary modern return of Christ, G. A. Studdert-Kennedy wrote, in his famous poem, *Indifference,*

When Jesus came to Golgotha they hanged Him on a tree,
They drave great nails in hands and feet, and made a Calvary;
They crowned Him with a crown of thorns; red were his
    wounds and deep,
For those were crude and cruel days, and human flesh
    was cheap.
When Jesus came to Birmingham, they simply passed Him by;
They never hurt a hair of Him, they only let Him die;
For men had grown more tender and they would not
    give Him pain;
They only just passed down the street, and left Him in the rain.

You needn't really wonder what people would do *if* Jesus came, for He *has*, in effect, visited every community that has heard the Gospel:
"God . . . in these last days has spoken to us *in His Son*" (Heb. 1:1-2).

What do most people *do* about Christ? What do most professing Christians *do* about Him? Sadly enough, most people—religious or otherwise—do little or nothing. Multitudes, inside and outside of our churches, pay lip service to the idea of Christ but think and live as though He did not exist. Perhaps they call on Him in times of acute crisis, in the half-hearted hope that He will intervene and help them. But when things are going well—when they enjoy reasonable health, when their income keeps up with the cost of living, when their chances for advancement look good, and when they are making friends with the "right" people —they are likely to ignore God or forget about Him.

If you want God's good life, take Him into account in *everything*. He is interested in *all* you do, and is able to help you under *all* circumstances. In our Scripture for this unit, James mentions three *specific* ways in which you are to take God into account: in how you talk about people (4:11-12); in your planning for the future (4:13-17); and in your attitude toward money (5:1-6).

God and How You Talk about People (James 4:11-12)
For the third time (cf. 1:26; 3:1-12), James deals with how men use and misuse the gift of speech. This repetition shows the importance he attaches to talk, the most common everyday activity. He warns us not to "talk against" other Christians. What leads a Christian to "talk against" another person? (4:11) Under what circumstances would *you* be tempted to commit this sin? (73)

Some people are born with easy-going dispositions. They aren't inclined to say a word against anyone. Others tend by nature to indulge in incessant chatter and gossip—even in slander or backbiting. Some people's circumstances tempt them to "speak against" others. If they feel inferior or jealous, or if they are not accepted by their peers, they may attack others' reputations in a futile, sinful effort to compensate. They may vent their disappointment or hard feelings—which are often justified—in truthful but unkind criticism. They may resort to the dangerous boomerang of malicious gossip. As we noted in unit 6, it would be hard to say how many reputations have been ruined, homes broken up, hopes blasted, and lives blighted by cruel and unnecessary talk. And all too 'often, the individuals who do the talking hurt themselves far worse than they hurt the people they attack. They become known as character assassins, and fewer and fewer people trust or confide in them.

It is a sin to speak against another Christian, writes James:

1. To speak evil against a fellow believer is, usually, to condemn him.

2. To condemn a brother is to exercise the function of a judge.

3. To take over the function of a judge not only implies that God is inadequate in *His* judging, but violates Jesus' command to "judge not" (Matt. 7:1). Only God (James 4:12), who is "able to save and to destroy," has authority to judge. Only God knows *all* about *everyone*. When *you* judge a person, by criticizing or "talking against" him, you do so on insufficient evidence. You act on partial knowledge—and without authority to enforce your judgment.

If you take God into account in speaking about other people, you allow *Him* to do the judging. If others wrong you or speak evil of you, you commit them and their words to *Him*. Instead of repaying them in kind, you pray for them.

Someone asked a placid old church sexton how he managed to keep his temper in spite of all the unreasonable and often contradictory demands made on him by the people in the church. "Oh," he replied, "I just puts my feelings in neutral and lets them shove me around." If you rely on the Lord, you will resist the impulse to defend yourself against those who are unfair to you, accuse you falsely, or talk maliciously about you. Keep your mind on what God expects of *you* and you will be so busy that you will not be critical about others.

Too few Christians live this way. It is more comfortable to disapprove of others than to keep oneself approved in God's sight. We feel "big" when we view the shortcomings of others and small when we look at our own.

God's Will and Planning for the Future (James 4:13-17)

Sometimes members of a church committee meet to decide an important issue. They talk for two hours and then close with a brief "word of prayer" asking God to bless the decisions they have reached. Would it not be much more logical for them to pray first, asking God to lead them to right conclusions?

Aren't we all somewhat like these committee members? Day after day, we are preparing for the future in one way or another. Often we do not take God into account at all—except that now and then, when we think of it, we may ask Him to bless whatever we are doing today or have decided to do tomorrow.

Most secular businessmen make little or no pretense of taking God into account in their planning. They depend for their success on such legitimate aids as management consultants, business analyses, and shrewd judgment. Why do you think, then, that Christians should remember God's will in business and personal planning?

(74)

You probably suggested more than one reason for considering God in planning for the future. God knows the end from the beginning, and is never surprised by what develops. He takes into account all the factors about which you can only guess. He can enable you to plan ahead wisely.

But, James says, consult God not only because you need His

foreknowledge, but because of the extreme brevity and uncertainty of human life: "You are just a vapor that appears for a little while and then vanishes away" (v. 14). You cannot command a single moment of the uncertain tomorrow.

If you are a young adult, you may find this truth hard to accept. You are strong of body, your mind is keen and alert, and life stretches ahead of you as a long succession of challenging years. When you were a child, a day seemed as long as a week, and a month as long as a year. Now time moves more rapidly, but as yet you probably have little awareness of how, when you are much older, the years will melt away and the sand remaining in life's glass will run out at an ever-faster rate. As a poet has put it,

> The years slip by like grace notes in a song;
> Only the days and nights are ever long.

Life is *brief*, but God is eternal. Only He can enable you to use to best advantage whatever time He puts at your disposal. Only He can invest your life with the element of permanence. Only He can put eternity in your heart.

Life is *uncertain*, too. "You do not know what your life will be like tomorrow" (v. 14), let alone next month or next year. So it is the height of presumption for you to assume that you'll be able to carry out all your plans (v. 13). A careless or drunken driver, a criminal on the prowl, a sudden attack of serious illness, the death of someone else, or a memo advising you that your services are no longer required by your employer—these are only a few possibilities. A 101 other unexpected developments are daily changing, with disconcerting suddenness, the courses of thousands of lives. How do you know *you* won't be next?

How would acting on the advice of verse 15 affect your life?
(75)

It is *wise* to make careful plans. God gave you intelligence so that you can act wisely and discreetly. But it is arrogant (v. 16) to plan for the uncertain future, which may be much briefer or longer than you expect, without taking God into account. One gets the impression that the people about whom James wrote were *proud* of their self-made arrangements, made without regard for God and His will.

What are some of the decisions facing people like you in which it is important to consider God's will?
(76)

Don't be fearful of making plans and decisions but, as you make them, don't be too "final" about them. Keep in mind that your plans are subject to God's interruptions and alterations. Such an attitude will avoid your being crushed or upset if the Lord sees fit to change your plans. Most Christians give mental assent to God's sovereignty in their lives, but practice little *conscious* submission to Him in making plans, schedules, and the like. For example, you may have set your heart on going to a certain vacation spot—but as you look ahead to your haven of rest, be ready to accept graciously, without resentment, any changes the Lord makes necessary. And as you think about a prospective investment, buying a new car, or taking a new job in another area, consider not only the common-sense factors on which non-Christians base their judgment, but the all-important matter of God's leading.

In giving you the guidance you look for, the Lord may not bring to your mind a verse of Scripture that bears on your plans. It is not at all probable that He will send an angel to counsel you in a dream or a vision. He is much more likely to give you a quiet conviction about the course of action you should follow, and perhaps He will confirm it with various circumstantial developments.

"I have showed you what is right to do, and any failure to do

so on your part is sin" (v. 17, Moffatt), our chapter concludes. It is not enough to *know* that you should take God's will into account. You must actually *do* so, or you are sinning. This same principle applies to all of life. You sin whenever you do what you shouldn't do, but you also sin when you don't do what you know you ought to. Can you suggest a few of the things Christians know they ought to do which they often leave undone?
(77)

God and Your Attitude toward Money (James 5:1-6)
Don't be quick to ignore the next six verses of James as though they applied only to people with huge fortunes. Many of the men about whom James wrote in this passage were no better off than a majority of modern believers in the United States, Canada, or England. Standards of living in the first century were painfully lower than in our respective western affluent societies.

James was writing to people who had more than they *needed* of this world's goods. Few people *admit* they have more than they need—but most of us are in this category if we have savings accounts, savings and loan shares, or stocks and bonds. How do we know, from this passage, that the writer is not talking to *all* rich people?
(78)

It would be a mistake to say that God is "down" on the rich. It does seem, though, as if the possession of wealth is often likely to add a dimension of complexity to one's life. It is no sin to own property and to have a large bank account. What *were* the faults of the rich men against whom James wrote in this section?

(79)

Plainly, James did not condemn these men for being wealthy. He condemned them for the way they had acquired their money and for what they were doing with it. Wealth honestly come by and wisely used is a blessing to its owners and to those it helps. But the rich men to whom James wrote left much to be desired in how they got their fortunes and in what they did with them.

What do the terms "rotted . . . moth-eaten . . . rusted" (vv. 2-3) suggest to you about the wealth of the rich men whom James addressed?

(80)

Every so often you read about some "pauper" who dies in a shack on the edge of the city dump. When the emaciated corpse, dressed in dirty rags, is found, and his rat-infested shanty is torn down, workmen discover $52,472 in small-denomination bills tucked away in the poor creature's lumpy mattress. Instead of using his money to make himself and other people comfortable, the wretch stashed it away where it helped neither him nor anyone else.

"Never possess anything," advised the late A. W. Tozer. "Have it, and use it, but never lay claim to it as yours." Money is to be *used*. Christians are to be provident about the future, but James seems to condemn storing up money at compound interest merely to "rust" and become "moth-eaten" while people suffer for lack of what it could do for them. When a man *hoards* his money, he doesn't possess it—it possesses him. It will be a testimony against him in the day of judgment (v. 3), and he may well weep and howl because of the miseries ahead of him (v. 1). James' prophecy was literally fulfilled a few years later at the destruction of Jerusalem, when many rich people were put to death and their hoarded wealth was seized by the Romans.

If you had a large fortune, how would you go about using it wisely?

(81)

Most people think of wealth as the first step toward the good life. Money can buy you things and make your circumstances pleasant, but it is not true (cf. p. 8) that money can buy happiness. In order to use money, little or much, wisely, you must take God into account. You must recognize that you are a steward of what you have, and that both your time and your money really belong to Him. As you obey Him in using them, you will make better lives possible for others and, in so doing, will enjoy God's good life more richly yourself.

God is not nearly so much concerned with what you would do with the million dollars you don't have as He is with how you use the ten dollars in your pocket. "If the readiness [to give] is present, it is acceptable according to what a man has, not according to what he does not have" (2 Cor. 8:12).

Some rich men merely fail to use their money for worthy needs; some spend it selfishly on themselves and their own pleasure (v. 5). They live luxuriously at a time when poorer people within reach are starving to death for lack of life's necessities. In the face of the extreme poverty in many parts of the world today, with multitudes going to bed hungry every night, do *you* think a Christian is justified in building himself a $100,000 house or in spending $5,000 for a car or hundreds of dollars for a fur piece? Defend your answer.

(82)

A good deal may be said on both sides of this question. Wealthy Christians may defend the practice of living on a level appropriate to their incomes. In this setting, they believe, they can make contacts with a class of people often not reached for Christ by evangelicals in modest circumstances. They may also point out that by spending their money lavishly they are supporting the economy and making jobs available for many workers. Be careful not to condemn a person—even if you don't see things his way—who is living in accordance with what he sincerely believes is right (cf. Rom. 14:4, 10, 12). In the last analysis, how a person uses his money is a question which he must settle with God, to whom he will give an account.

James censured rich men who acquired their wealth by exploiting other people. These wealthy employers withheld the wages of their workers (v. 4). Either they did not pay them at all or, more likely, they paid them at sub-standard rates. Conditions like this are not nearly as common today as they were before labor unions turned the tables and assured most workers of their rights (sometimes with unfairness to employers!). However, there are still many workers, even in the United States, who are grossly underpaid. The migrant workers who follow the crops, for example, are not covered by minimum wage laws, have no "fringe benefits," live in fearfully squalid housing, and must bring up their children with few educational or other advantages.

There has always been—and probably always will be—tension between the haves and the have-nots, between management and labor. We may be sure that whenever men take an undue share of the profits of an undertaking at the expense of those who engage in the venture with them, God is displeased. The Lord may be temporarily silent about such injustice, but He hears the cries of those who are being oppressed (v. 4b).

Taking God into Account in All of Life (Summary)
Looking back over this extremely practical passage, notice its teaching on everyday attitudes and actions.

1. To speak against other Christians may be taking on yourself God's right to pass judgment on them.

2. Human life is brief and tomorrow is always uncertain.

3. The better part of discretion is to seek the all-wise Lord's will concerning personal or business plans for the future.

4. It is not enough to know what is right. Not to *do* what you know is right is to commit sin.

5. Your present possessions are no assurance of your future happiness.

6. If you are getting rich at the expense of other people, you are incurring the judgment of God.

7. It is prudent to prepare for the future, but wrong to hoard money that should be put to work.

8. You will give an accounting to God if you use your money on selfish extravagances when you could be helping those who lack life's necessities.

Think and Do

How different are you from a non-Christian in the way you talk about other people? In the way you plan for the future? In how you make and spend your money? What are some of the specific ways in which you will be more careful to take God's will into account in these practical matters? What will you do differently this week as a result of your study? When will you begin?

PATIENCE AND THE LORD'S RETURN

James 5:7-12

"Be patient; strengthen your hearts; for the coming of the Lord is at hand" (James 5:8).

Unbelievers scoff at the idea that Christ will return, but can you suggest a few reasons why few *Christians* appear to be keenly interested, these days, in the Second Coming, His "glorious appearing"?
(83)

The return of Christ was a cardinal doctrine of the Early Church. Jesus Himself promised His disciples that He would return for them (John 14:3). Shortly after He ascended bodily to heaven, an angel told them they would see Him come back "in just the same way" (Acts 1:11).

The first Christians believed Christ would return at any time. They expected to be alive when He came. As the years turned into decades and the decades into centuries, however, Jesus' disappointed followers began to explain away His promise to come back. Some said it had already been fulfilled at Pentecost: Jesus *had* come back, in the person of the Holy Spirit. Others believed the promise meant He would return for each believer at the moment of death. More and more, Christians spiritualized away what they had at first taken as a literal promise that Christ would come again.

If you take the Bible as meaning what it says, you will find that it speaks firmly and frequently about the Lord's return, a major event in God's program for the consummation of human history.

In the last chapter of his epistle, James says the Lord's coming is a glorious event for God's people to anticipate (James 5:7-8) and that it involves a judgment they are to avoid (v. 9). He also gives them a splendid example to follow (vv. 10-11) and tells them about a practice to shun (v. 12).

A Glorious Event to Anticipate (James 5:7-8)

Try your hand at a homemade definition of the word "patient": (84)

Webster defines "patient" as bearing trials without complaint; expectant with calmness or without discontent; undisturbed by obstacles, delays, and failures. Until *when* does James say Christians are to be patient, and *why*? (85)

Our Lord was an example of patience, and we are to be like Him. Patience, too, is part of the fruit of the Spirit (Gal. 5:22-23), and therefore Christians are to exhibit this quality. Another motive for patience is given in James 5:8: The Lord's coming is "at hand." It will put an end to all the trials that test you. You may therefore stop worrying and fretting about them *right now*. His coming, your "blessed hope" (Titus 2:13)—the event on which your anticipation is focused—may occur at any given moment.

How *long* are you to be patient? "Until the coming of the Lord" (v. 7), says James. From what you know about the Early

Church, how did the expectation of the Lord's early return affect the daily lives of Christians?
(86)

If you had the use of a million dollars for only two weeks, what would you do with it? Of course you would spend it as fast as you could, buying whatever you need or want. If you knew for certain that your life would end at the Lord's coming two weeks from now, what would you do? If you are a believer, you would probably do as early Christians did. Because they believed firmly that Christ would return at any moment, they poured out their lives lavishly in His service. Their primary concern was not the acquisition of a comfortable suburban ranch home, two cars, color TV, and a complete set of modern household appliances. They were not much concerned with climbing the social ladder and keeping ahead of the folks next door.

The early Christians' chief concern was with spiritual things—with knowing Christ, with growing in their communion with God, and with telling others about the Saviour. They lived for eternity. To be sure, there were hypocrites among them, and carnal believers who were materialistic and earthbound, and backsliders who had lost the vision. But we are forced to conclude that the amount of true spirituality in the Early Church was greater than it has been at any time since—and infinitely greater than it is today. The difference may perhaps be largely credited to the early believers' burning hope for the Lord's coming. They hailed this event as the answer to their needs and the climax of their joy. Today some Christians are so happy in their worldliness and materialism that they would actually weep if they knew Christ were returning next week.

Even if you have never studied what the Bible teaches about the Second Coming, try an answer to this question: What are some of the happenings or events that *you* associate with the return of Christ?

(87)

Would you like to review briefly some of the interpretations of the return of Christ that have developed over the centuries? There are three principal views, and they center around what people think about the Millennium. This word means "thousand years" and refers to the reign of Christ and His people on earth (Rev. 20:4-7). Here are the three views:

1. *Postmillennialism.* This position was held for centuries and is usually considered the traditional view of the Church. Its followers say the "thousand years" is a figurative expression and represents merely a long period of indefinite duration. They hold that the efforts of the Church will gradually improve social, economic, international, and other conditions until man's history culminates in a long time ("thousand years") of peace, prosperity, and spirituality, during which Christ will reign on earth *in the hearts of His people.* This period, they say, will be climaxed by the return of Christ to judge the living and the dead. The righteous will then be taken with Him to heaven and the unrighteous will be cast into hell.

World events since 1914 have not encouraged belief that the world is getting better and better. For the most part, people have abandoned this view as unrealistic.

2. *Amillennialism.* Friends of this position teach that the world is not getting better and better, but worse and worse. This trend will continue, they say, until human history is climaxed by the return of Christ to judge the living and the dead. The "thousand years" is merely a symbolic figure, they tell us, that refers to the long reign of God's people with Christ in heaven.

3. *Premillennialism.* This position, which its advocates maintain was the viewpoint of the Early Church, holds that world conditions will continue to worsen and that they will culminate in seven years of great tribulation. Immediately prior to the Tribulation, according to the interpretation of many evangelicals,

Christ will come to raise the bodies of the believing dead; He will transform the bodies of living believers (1 Thess. 4:13-17; 1 Cor. 15:52). He and His people, after the seven-year period, will then reign on this earth for a thousand years of righteousness, peace, and prosperity, after which the wicked dead will be judged and the eternal kingdom set up.

There are difficulties in connection with each of these views, but some feel that the premillennial position accounts more satisfactorily for a number of passages that are extremely puzzling if one follows either of the other two interpretations. It should be mentioned that though premillennialism is the favorite interpretation among evangelicals, not all evangelical Christians are premillenarian.

Some modern critics charge that the whole idea of the Second Coming is of comparatively recent origin. This notion is so flagrantly out of line with New Testament teachings that it hardly merits serious consideration. Christians began looking for the Lord's return on the very day He ascended into heaven (Acts 1:11).

Why do you think most people—and some Christians—refuse to believe in Christ's second coming?
(88)

The Bible sets no dates for Christ's return, other than to say that it is "at hand." He could return at any moment. He will come when He is least expected (Luke 12:40). Judging from the naturalistic trends in modern thought, the new morality, the "God is dead" theology, and the like, most people today have no expectation of any event so supernatural as Christ's bodily return. Their skepticism, of course, fulfills the very condition Jesus mentioned (cf. also Luke 18:8).

When the Lord returns, we shall see a general resumption of God's direct supernatural dealings with human beings. God has been active in human history right along, but he has *generally* worked through men and "natural" phenomena. We do not imply that in the coming judgment God may not work, at least in part, through human beings, but we must not restrict Him. For example, He may well use the fearful power of nuclear fission to implement some of the devastating judgments described in The Revelation—but His omnipotence far outreaches anything The Bomb could unleash.

Verses 7-8 deal with the blessings, rather than the judgments, associated with Christ's second coming. After His return His people will no longer be victims of injustice, graft, corruption, crime, immorality, discrimination, disappointment, illness, death, sorrow, loneliness, frustration, or any other evil thing. All believers will be with Christ (John 14:3). They will be made like Him, and will see Him as He is (1 John 3:2). Their bodies of weakness and corruption will be made like His glorious resurrection body (Phil. 3:20-21). Physical imperfections and limitations will be gone forever.

Because this wonderful personal transformation and eternal environment await you, "Be patient." Put up with injustice, hardship, inconvenience, unpleasantness, and persecution. Accept whatever the Lord allows to come your way, knowing that a single moment of future glory will erase from your mind forever all you remember of earth's sorrows.

Cultivate God's viewpoint on life and eternity. Imagine a piece of string several yards in length, stretched taut, with a small knot at one end. If you look along that string from the unknotted end, you will barely see the knot. This view illustrates man's outlook. The long string is life, and eternity is the tiny knot, hardly noticeable, at the far end.

Now put your eye at the knotted end of the string. This is how God sees things—the knot is human life and the long string is eternity. Life, to God, by contrast with eternity, is extremely brief. If you keep the knotted string in mind, it will help you to evaluate both time and eternity properly.

A farmer plants his seed and then "waits for the precious produce of the soil, being patient about it" (v. 7). Have you ever put in a vegetable garden? Gardening is a long-term project.

After you pat the soil into place over the seeds, all you can do is water it and, after the plans appear, cultivate—and wait. You are more or less at the mercy of the rain, the sun, and such creatures as the cutworm, the crow, and the ubiquitous bunny. From six to ten weeks after you plant, you *may* reap a crop. But there is no element of risk about Christ's return. God, who cannot lie, has promised it.

When General Douglas MacArthur left Bataan in 1942, he promised, "I shall return," and return he did. The Lord Jesus Christ said, "I will come again." Since He is the Son of God, we may depend on Him to do it. Our part is to be patient and faithful until He gets here.

A Condemnation to Avoid (James 5:9)

Chapter 5 begins with James' warning to the rich profiteers who were exploiting poor Christians in order to enrich themselves. Review, in brief, what James tells rich men in those verses.
(89)

Why, according to verse 9, is the Lord's coming a good reason for Christians not to complain?
(90)

A complaining, murmuring, discontented spirit is sinful. God will judge it. This judgment will occur at the Lord's return. The Judge is now "standing right at the door" (v. 9). Obviously, it is advisable to get rid of the spirit of complaining, at all costs. Be satisfied with such things as you have (Heb. 13:5). Look for your highest happiness not in your circumstances, possessions, or friends, but in your relationship with God.

You may think that while you have youth, health, and perhaps means, you'll enjoy the "good life" of self-indulgence and then, when you get old, you'll turn to the Lord and enjoy *Him*. Don't count on it! A person who lets other things crowd out enjoyment of God in earlier years is likely to find, when he no longer has the things and people that occupy his life, that he cannot easily fill the empty places with sudden enjoyment of spiritual realities.

A Wonderful Example for You to Follow (James 5:10-11)
Do you consider yourself a patient individual? If not, in what ways are you impatient?
(91)

The example of suffering and patience to which James refers you is "the prophets who spoke in the name of the Lord." God's messengers, in every age, have traveled a hard road. On the whole, they have not been well received. In His parable of the vineyard (Luke 20), Jesus pointed out that the tenants the vineyard owner had left in charge mistreated the servants sent them. They killed the owner's son. The parable was a graphic denunciation of the way God's people had mistreated His prophets and would crucify our Lord. According to tradition, Jeremiah was stoned in Egypt and a wicked king had Isaiah sawed in half. Stephen also was stoned. James and Paul were beheaded. All the apostles except John were martyred.

All these men had been in God's service. They had faithfully proclaimed His message, but they had to stand alone—and die alone. Their high and holy calling did not exempt them from suffering and martyrdom. Why should *you* expect freedom from hardship and tribulation?

Jack and Jane, childhood sweethearts, were married last year. Their families are both wealthy, and Jack's father has staked him to a lucrative business and a comfortable home. He and Jane have everything a couple could wish for—a lovely house, many friends, good health, a substantial income, and a fine baby boy. They never complain about anything. Since they "endure" their

situation, aren't they "blessed" (v. 11) for being patient?
(92)

No, there's nothing very noble in "enduring" circumstances as comfortable as most of us enjoy. For a good example of patient endurance, think about Job. He was a godly man, even if he was a bit inclined to self-righteousness. As you probably know, Job lost everything he had—possessions, family, and health. In addition to all the discomfort that went with his losses, he had to endure the critical comments of three wretched "friends." They hinted broadly that God would never have treated him so harshly if he had not been hiding a lot of secret sins. But Job learned, in due time, that "the Lord is full of compassion and is merciful" (v. 11).

How could a compassionate and merciful God allow a good man like Job to suffer? How can a compassionate God allow war and crime and immorality and starvation?

Men are responsible for most of the sin and misery against which they so bitterly protest. God created a good world. If only men had obeyed Him, crime, war, immorality, and the like would never have come into being. Don't blame God, then, for man's sin and its consequences. Of course, God could have made man incapable of sinning—but who would want to be a robot?

Maybe you ask why God doesn't put a stop to wrong by judging those who commit unrighteousness. God *will* do this in His own time. The parable of the wheat and the tares (Matt. 13:24-30) tells how God will handle the situation. God "is full of compassion and is merciful," and even in the time of judgment He will protect His people.

Remember Job's experience if you aren't getting ahead financially as rapidly as you would like, or if your neighbors are unfair or troublesome, or if sickness or an accident has come your way. Keep in mind Job's sublime faith (Job 13:15; 23:10) and the Lord's tenderness. Commit yourself and your circumstances to God, and be assured that He *still* does all things well (cf. Mark 7:37).

An Undesirable Practice for You to Avoid (James 5:12)

Verse 12 doesn't seem to be very strongly linked to the first 11 verses of chapter 5. It is another reference to the sins of speech which James mentions so often (1:19, 26; 3:2-12, 14; 4:11-12). Perhaps the writer brings up the subject here because some of his readers, in their excitement over oppression and apparent injustice, were reinforcing their language with oaths. This is a practice in which Christians are not to indulge (cf. Matt. 5:34-37).

Some Christians apply these prohibitions to oaths in a court of law. Most, though, feel James was forbidding the expressions people sometimes use when they want their hearers to be certain they are sincere in what they are saying. A Christian's bare word is to be enough. He is never to be like the youth, who, when he hadn't cut the lawn as he had said he would, objected to his father's reprimand. "I didn't *promise* to do it," he alibied.

"His word is his bond" is a complimentary remark never heard of a person who feels he must add an oath for emphasis whenever he wants to make sure people will believe him.

Patience and the Lord's Second Coming (Summary)

Now, for the important truths in James 5:7-12:

1. Christians are to be patient until the Lord's return.

2. They are to be patient because he is at hand to judge those who have been oppressing them.

3. They are to avoid wrong attitudes that the Lord will condemn.

4. The prophets of old are examples of patience; the farmer waiting for his crop is an illustration of it.

Think and Do

If you were convinced that the Lord were returning in a week, what would you do? What changes, if any, would you make in your attitude or conduct? Would you right any wrong relationships? Would you confess any sins to God? Would you witness to some of your acquaintances? How would you use your remaining time? Your money?

The Lord probably will not return in one week—but He may! God warns you, "Be ready . . . for the Son of Man is coming at an hour when you do not think He will" (Matt. 24:44).

Try for a greater measure of mildness in your speech. Seek the happiness experienced only by one who, though he may not fully understand God's purposes, depends on the Lord's compassion and mercy. The truly happy person is one who is steadfast, not disturbed by every changing circumstance.

How about living for one week, beginning now, as you would like the Lord to find you living at His return? Will you accept the challenge of such a week? If you do, you may never again be satisfied with anything less!

UNIT **10**

THE POWER OF PRAYER

James 5:13-20

"The effective prayer of a righteous man can accomplish much" (James 5:16b).

To be able to pick up a telephone and talk with any one of millions of persons, in this country or abroad, is a communications miracle of considerable dimensions. You would certainly miss the telephone if you had to do without it, but there is one form of communication of which you may fail to make full use. Even more simple than direct distance dialing, and without the expense involved even in night-rate telephone service, is prayer. By it you are privileged to talk to Almighty God about your interests, problems and needs.

A little girl, meaning to express the permanence of God's sovereignty in a familiar evangelical cliché, said, "God is still on the phone!" There are times when people you try to reach by telephone do not answer. There are times when God *seems* not to hear. You may be certain, however, that He "is still on the phone"—and that He hears every word you say to Him.

Before you begin to study what James has to say, write here the reasons why most Christians, in your opinion, do so little praying: (93)

People tell jokes about the unmarried woman who lectures on child raising and about the seedy-looking failure who peddles books on how to succeed in business. People who talk or speak eloquently about prayer have not necessarily done much praying. This is not true of James, who speaks out of much personal experience. According to tradition, his knees were as hard as a camel's because he spent so much time kneeling in prayer.

Some Christians do not pray because they are not living in fellowship with God. Some are too busy with temporal things. Some are ignorant of God's promise to answer their petitions. Some have too small a conception of Him and what He will do—they do not believe He is really an active force in life.

James, in his most practical of epistles, has already told you that God is ready to answer your request for wisdom if you ask in faith (James 1:5-6), and that you may lack some blessings because you either fail to ask God for them or ask out of selfish motives (4:2-3). In the concluding paragraph of his letter, James deals with praying in times of sorrow and joy (5:13) and sickness (vv. 14-16); with the example of a man who prayed effectively (vv. 17-18); and with intercession for people who have spiritual needs (vv. 19-20).

Many Christians believe God is always with them. They count on His resources and turn to Him in emergencies. They rarely pray, however, when things are going well. Their relationship with God is like that of a husband and wife who live together but never engage in conversation unless an emergency threatens, merely accepting one another's presence and never communicating in words!

Sharing Your Sorrows and Joys with God (James 5:13)

You will probably admit that you have your ups and downs. Some days are sunny and others are rainy. There are times when you are sitting on Cloud 9—wherever that is. There are times when you are in the Slough of Despond.

Don't be satisfied with "life on the lowest plane"! And God did not intend His children to put up with a sort of roller-coaster up-and-down experience, either. The good life is one of continual rejoicing (Phil. 4:4). Christians, as we have seen, must expect their share of problems, troubles, illness, and affliction, but *they can be joyful* even in difficulty. How? "Is anyone among you suffering?" asks James. "Let him pray" (v. 13).

How would prayer help a believer who is suffering?
(94)

If you are like most people, you long to share your troubles—your fears, doubts, sorrows, and pains—with someone who loves you and cares about you. Even if your friend can't lend you the money you need, or relieve your pain, or advise you, you find comfort and strength in his love and concern.

God loves you more than any human being possibly could. "It matters to Him about you" (1 Pet. 5:7, free trans.). More than that, God is all-wise and all-powerful. He is able to do more for you than any conceivable earthly friend. He is the God of all comfort (2 Cor. 1:3). He has every resource (Phil. 4:19); He wants to be the Strength of your life (Ps. 27:1).

In the Bible, God talks to you. In prayer, for the most part, you talk to God. Prayer is God's antidote for sorrow. You will find, in addition to His answers, a marvelous therapy simply in unburdening yourself to your heavenly Father. He knows all about you, to be sure, but He wants and asks you to share your problems with Him. As you take Him your burdens, perplexities, losses, and heartaches, you will find yourself strengthened and encouraged, enabled to go on your way rejoicing in the One who is working all things together for your good (cf. Rom. 8:28).

And when you feel *cheerful*, don't forget God. Rather, "sing praises"! (Actually *singing*, by the way, is worth a try!)

What effect will "singing praises" have on a cheerful Christian? On other nearby Christians? On unbelievers?
(95)

Verse 13 implies, then, that your entire life is to be centered in God. When you are discouraged, ask His help. When you feel cheerful, thank Him for His goodness. This amounts to keeping in touch with Him at all times. Prayer and praise are to be the overall attitudes of your personal Christian life:

> Prayer is the Christian's vital breath,
> The Christian's native air.

One of the finest devotional aids available is the Book of Psalms. It has been said that in the psalms every emotion of the human heart is perfectly expressed. Read through the psalms, marking those that deal with doubt, fear, jealousy, love, concern, happiness, sorrow, repentance, bewilderment, rejoicing, and other emotions of which you are conscious. A Bible so marked will be an invaluable devotional aid for the rest of your life.

Perhaps you think, "But I don't feel any different after I pray." God does not *ask* you to feel different, nor does He *promise* that you will. The absence of feelings does not in any way alter the fact that God hears every word you say to Him. It does not detract from His ability to do what is best for you. Feelings may come, in time—but their absence is not important. Depend on God's character and promises—*not* on *your* feelings.

Pray to God in Time of Sickness (James 5:14-16)

When Jesus returns to earth (cf. unit 9), a believer's body will be changed and made like Christ's glorious body. That transformation will mark the end of all sickness and pain. Why do you think it is reasonable, in the meantime, for Christians to believe that the Lord heals their bodies?

(96)

Some people seem to feel that a Christian who believes in the healing power of God is a fanatic, but the Bible records many cases of supernatural healing and plainly teaches that God's people have a right to look to Him for it. Jesus, while on earth, sent out His disciples to teach *and to heal.* Though the command to heal is absent from the Great Commission, healings were among the signs that were to follow those who believed. God commands you to present your body to Him (Rom. 12:1). If you have done this sincerely, your body *belongs* to God. Is it not logical, then, for you to expect Him to care for it?

What are we to think when healing does not follow our prayer for the sick?

(97)

Some Christian doctors say they have never seen a healing that did not result from natural causes. Others testify that God has supernaturally intervened in sicknesses under their observation. Many Christians know, from personal experience, that God has healed them—often in spectacular fashion. On the other hand, we must admit that God does not *always* heal. Absence of healing, however, is never due to lack of ability on God's part

Because He knows vastly more than we do, God has good and sufficient—if unrevealed—reasons for not complying with all our requests. Perhaps the unhealed sickness is God's hand in chastening, or His discipline for developing the sick person (or those around him) spiritually. You cannot always know *why* God allows sickness—but you can always be sure that His will for His people is good. When a sickness has served His purpose, God will deal with it—but don't assume that *you* know when God has accomplished His purpose.

James writes that a sick Christian was to send for the elders of the local church—men who by reason of age or experience were in leadership positions. These men were ready to help fellow believers by praying for them and giving them sympathetic advice. The elders were to pray over the sick person, anointing him with oil in the Lord's name. (This anointing is not the "extreme unction" of the Roman Catholic Church, which is administered only when death is expected.)

Why do you think it is wrong (or not wrong) for Christians to use "means," such as medicines or the services of a doctor, when they are sick?
(98)

The mention of oil (v. 14) hardly justifies the use of "means" in treating illness, for the next verse points out that "the prayer offered in faith [not the oil] will restore the sick, and *the Lord* will raise him up."

However—though we must respect those who think otherwise —it would seem logical, in fighting sickness, to use the medical discoveries God has enabled men to make. God may heal without use of means, but we limit His sovereignty if we insist that He *will* not heal supernaturally when means are used.

Over one of the pavilions in a large urban medical center is the inscription, "From the most High cometh healing." Unbelievers may use medicine without prayer. Christians may use prayer without medicine. Other believers may use prayer *and* medicine. But, in a way, it is always God who heals. He is our Maker. He is the Designer of the complex processes by which the sick body overcomes injury and disease. Moreover, it is clear from Scripture and from experience that God often intervenes and heals directly by supernatural power.

A medical school student was assured by his instructor, "Remember, when you are prescribing for a patient, that four out of five cases would get better without treatment." Whether a doctor and medicine are involved or not, *it is God who heals*— though some people prefer to credit "nature," which is a way of describing God at work.

We know from Jesus' words (John 9:3) that physical disability is not always a result of sin. Doctors tell us today that a large percentage of illness is psychosomatic—that is, it results from people's inability to cope with the pressures of modern life. But guilt feelings also cause illness, and James suggests (v. 15) that there may at times be a relationship between illness and past sins. God, however, stands ready to forgive a sick person.

However you explain it, the sick person you pray for may not recover any faster than you would normally expect him to had you not prayed. Sometimes, indeed, he does not get better at all, even when those who have interceded for him have had strong convictions that he would be healed.

In spite of the prayer that must have been offered for Trophimus, Paul left him sick at Miletum (2 Tim. 4:20). Many think Paul's thorn in the flesh (2 Cor. 12) was a physical disability about which he had prayed without experiencing healing. But though we tend to focus on the occasions when prayer seems to fail, we must not forget that God's normal intention, judging by what James writes, is to heal His people in response to believing prayer.

Verse 16 begins with a "therefore," which directs your attention to what precedes it. Since you have such glorious promises —the restoration of your sick body and the forgiveness of your guilty soul—confess your sins and pray for others! This verse, like the previous one, recognizes the possibility of a relationship between sin and sickness, for it links confession and healing.

The confession mentioned here is not the auricular confession of the Roman Catholic Church, which is always made to a priest. Nor does the passage sanction the confessional orgies that have been held by some cultic groups, with their wholesale recountings of sexual promiscuity or perversion. What harm could result from such general confession of personal sins?
(99)

In the light of the context, James may have had in view the confession of the sick person to the elder who came to pray. Such confession would enable the elder better to counsel the penitent. Confession may also be due someone you have harmed by your wrongdoing. For example, if you have told a lie that has embarrassed someone, you may owe him both a confession and an apology (cf. Matt. 5:23-24). But indiscriminate public confession is "like sowing germs of disease in the minds and lives of others" (McNab).

It should be pointed out, here, that many Christians today are finding rich blessing in meeting together regularly with small groups—not more than 12 or 15 people. The members of such groups become closely knit together in a wonderful spiritual fellowship. This relationship is conducive to frank and friendly sharing of insights and experiences (rather than *sins*) in a way that encourages mutual understanding and spiritual growth. Through the influence of such groups, many non-Christians are being won to Christ.

Don't be so taken up with the command to "confess your sins" (James 5:16) that you overlook the equally important command to "pray for one another." The subject of this whole passage is *prayer*, not confession. The final words emphasize this: "The effective *prayer* of a righteous man can accomplish much." To a righteous man—a believer who is living a holy life in close fellowship with God—prayer is *dynamic*. It works. It produces real, specific results. It does not change God's mind, but it is the means by which He has ordained to fulfill His purposes.

The Example of a Man Who Prayed (James 5:17-18)
People *talk* a lot about the weather, but *do* very little. Elijah was different. He actually *did* something about the weather! He brought on a drought that lasted more than three years, and then he prayed the rain back. For what reasons, from this passage, do you think James chose Elijah as a good example of how a believer can accomplish things through prayer?
(100)

Elijah (cf. 1 Kings 17–18) is a good example because a real miracle followed his petition. The drought did not coincide by happenstance with his prayer for it—he announced it ahead of time. He did the same with the rain that ended the long dry spell. Elijah prayed "earnestly." Much prayer is superficial or halfhearted. To pray earnestly is to pray with strong intention—to put one's entire heart into one's supplication.

Perhaps the best reason why Elijah is a good example of effective praying is that he was "a man with a nature like ours." Do you think God's servants stood on pedestals to which you may not aspire? They were human beings. They were susceptible to weakness and weariness. They were tempted to impatience, anger, and disappointment. Though Elijah was sincere and godly, he was human, too—and when he prayed, God answered. The implication is that God will hear *you*, too, if you pray as earnestly as Elijah did.

Intercession for People with Spiritual Needs (James 5:19-20)
The Browns and the Grays have long been friends. Both go to the same church. Lately the Grays have become irregular in their church attendance. They tell the Browns about their "interesting" talks with local Jehovah's Witnesses. Just what (give details) should the Browns do?
(101)

There are many "orthodox" Christians who simply cross off their list—at times with satisfaction—Christians who have "wandered from the truth." Many Christians long for the joy of winning the lost to Christ, but overlook the joy in helping wayward believers. It is a Christian's duty to try to "turn back" a fellow believer who "strays from the truth" (v. 19). The Browns could do this through friendly counsel, helpful literature, and perhaps a suggestion to their pastor that he visit the Grays and lead them into a friendly, helpful discussion. Above all, the

Browns should be patient and loving. Any harshness or contempt might result in the Grays' leaving the church.

Prayer is not mentioned in verses 19 and 20, but in the context it is perhaps the chief means in view for the restoration of a wandering believer. Who is to say how many erring Christians have been brought back to the truth as the Holy Spirit has worked in response to the prayers of concerned believers?

What two results does James say will follow such intercessory prayer?

(102)

The text plainly states that the one who turns a sinner from his error "will save [the sinner's] soul from death." This could be a reference to the eternal death that results from sin—or to the physical death which God at times visits on sinning believers (1 Cor. 11:30). But the wanderer's sins will be covered by the precious blood of Christ as he returns from his disobedience and obeys the truth. There is no reference here to your being able to "cover" *your own* sins by helping others who have spiritual problems.

The Power of Prayer (Summary)

We have come to the end of our study of the good life that God makes possible to those who are His children through personal trust in the Lord Jesus Christ. In the closing paragraphs of his epistle, James makes these points:

1. Take your burdens and sorrows to God in prayer.

2. Praise Him for pleasant things that make life enjoyable.

3. Church leaders are to respond to the requests of sick Christians for intercessory prayer. They are to anoint such believers in the Lord's name.

4. Believing prayer can restore the sick as the Lord raises them up and forgives their sins.

5. Confess your sins to those whom you have wronged, and pray for needy Christians.

6. Elijah is an illustration of what a man who was "like us can accomplish through earnest prayer.

7. Intercede for those who have spiritual problems.

Think and Do

Is your praying "earnest"? Is it "offered in faith"? Does it "accomplish much"? If your answer to any of these questions is negative, what will you do in the way of correcting the situation?

Do you take your problems and sorrows to God in prayer? Do you thank Him heartily when things go well? Do you pray for the sick folk in your church? Is your prayer life deep and satisfying, or is it superficial and almost meaningless? What will you do differently about prayer as a result of this study? Will you take time each day, beginning tomorrow, to talk to God—even if you don't have the feeling that you are accomplishing anything?